Spare Room
TYCOON

To Rhoads Murphey

My teacher and friend

Spare Room
TYCOON

Succeeding Independently:
The 70 Lessons of
Sane Self-Employment

James Chan

NICHOLAS BREALEY
PUBLISHING

LONDON

First published by
Nicholas Brealey Publishing in 2000

36 John Street   1163 E. Ogden Avenue, Suite 705-229
London   Naperville
WC1N 2AT, UK   IL 60563-8535, USA
Tel: +44 (0)207 430 0224   Tel: (888) BREALEY
Fax: +44 (0)207 404 8311   *Fax: (630) 898 3595*
http://www.nbrealey-books.com
http://www.spareroomtycoon.com

ISBN 1-85788-247-4 (HB)

British Library Cataloguing in Publication Data
A catalogue record for this book is available from the
British Library.

Contents

I Am a
Spare Room Tycoon

I use a staircase to commute to my second-floor office from my third-floor bedroom or my first-floor kitchen. My company, Asia Marketing and Management, has global ambitions but consists largely of me and the intelligence, experience, contacts, and personality I bring to my clients' tasks.

I enjoy what I do, and I do it well. My work engages and surprises me. I'm still learning about my business, just as I am learning new things about myself. Although my experience tells me what is likely to work in my business, I still feel free to experiment. It is, after all, *my* business.

My work is an act of imagination. I have created it as I have gone along. It is not surprising, then, that it fits me very well. I'm in business for myself so that I can be myself.

Recently, at the supermarket, I encountered someone I met when I was first starting out. After he marveled that I had survived all these years, he remarked, "You must be really rich." When I told him I wasn't, at least not by his Wharton School standards, he became almost contemptuous. "The only reason to be in business for yourself is to make lots and lots of money," he said, pushing his cart rapidly toward the fancy crackers. I was left standing where I was, scrutinizing both the broccoli and the way I have lived my life.

No, I'm no software billionaire. I may never be listed in the Forbes 400. But I have a career that is far more interesting and satisfying than any I can imagine as an employee. Though there have been some rocky times since I went into business on my own more than 17 years ago, I am happy with the path I have taken.

How can I call myself a tycoon, you may wonder, if I'm not fabulously wealthy? In fact, the word tycoon comes, as I do, from China. It refers to one who rules, a sovereign. The word came into English, by way of Japanese, at a time when business was becoming bigger and bigger, and it referred to a powerful executive, a captain of industry. I'm actually a captain of industry myself, though my craft is more like a rowboat than an ocean liner. My empire is small, but I do rule it. And I'd rather be captain of my dinghy than a junior officer on the *Titanic*.

Every day, I meet more and more people who either aspire to be on their own, or are actually in business for themselves. In 1999, the *Wall Street Journal* reported that 8000 new businesses were opening in US homes each week, despite a full-employment economy. And in many other countries the trend is even more advanced. A 1998 Dartmouth College study found that self-employment in the 23 developed European, North American and Asian countries in the OECD averages between 19 and 23 percent.

The globalization of business seems to be producing a handful of transnational behemoths in every industry. But it is also giving individuals access to vast quantities of information and to communication technologies that allow a home office to be as well connected to the world as is a downtown office tower. It's therefore no surprise that many people with imagination and nerve feel that they can make a bigger impact as individuals than as functionaries in vast, anonymous organizations.

Many of those contemplating independence are people who have worked for large corporations and either fear that they are going to be displaced or find that this is actually happening to them. Others are younger people who appear to be on a career fast track, but who understand that every organization is unstable, and loyalty is largely irrelevant. People just out of school are likewise seeking ways to invent themselves so that they can prosper amid tumult and retain a sense of personal integrity. Parents are looking for ways to find the time to be part of their children's lives while they invent a business of their own. All sorts of people—women and men, old and young—are looking for ways to live while keeping soul and body together.

Some have dreams of making lots and lots of money—and none of them would mind if it happened. A few have dreams of creating large new companies, but many more don't share the common assumption that one must grow large or die. The great majority of people I meet would be happy to be mildly prosperous. Their main payoff comes in personal satisfaction, in autonomy, in deliverance from office politics, in the freedom to make their own mistakes instead of being forced to execute the misjudgments of others. Living by your wits can be risky, but it also makes you feel more fully alive.

Telling stories

Independent business people live intense but often lonely lives. It's easy to lose perspective, even to go a little crazy, when we have only ourselves to depend on. Knowing that other people have survived crises much like those we face can help keep us sane.

That is why, when we independents get together, we tell each other stories. Many of these are lamentations about customers who demand the impossible by next Wednesday, but take forever to pay for it. Some are lessons of persistence rewarded, as a long-cultivated prospect comes through with a big order. Some are cautionary tales of opportunity practically breaking down the door while the self-employed person, misunderstanding what she has to offer, assumes that the opportunity is not hers. There are many stories of happy accidents, of chance encounters and offhand remarks that lead to new work and new ideas for making a better living.

I like to hear these stories, and to tell them too. They teach important lessons not only about how to make money on your own, but also how to survive the emotional challenges of running a business. They offer reassurance that I'm really not alone. Indeed, although my business is an unusual one, when I hear engineers, financiers, lawyers, artists, building contractors, computer entrepreneurs, writers, recruiters, and many others telling their stories, it is clear that all sorts of self-employed people are seeking similar satisfactions and must overcome most of the same anxieties. It is easy to drive yourself crazy while trying to make a business succeed. Hearing of other people's experiences helps me to set my own boundaries between my work and my life, to strive for balance and to remind myself that I'm trying to make a living, not kill myself.

Spare room tycoons are an astonishingly diverse group of people. We are, after all, people who feel compelled to express our individuality through running our own businesses. What we do is shaped by very different ideas of who we are, what we want to be, and how we want to live our lives. There is no one recipe for successful self-employment. Each one of us is starting with a completely different set of ingredients. And each is hoping for a unique result.

Many spare room tycoons with whom I spoke see self-employment as an ethical choice, one that allows them to make promises they are able to keep. Others see their careers as a mission, an adventure, a struggle, or an accident.

Following an introductory chapter that offers a framework for thinking about being a spare room tycoon, the rest of this book consists mainly of real stories, taken from my own life and from interviews with other independents. With only one exception, all of the names are real. These are actual stories of independent business people, as seen from the inside.

Some of these stories are funny, or sad, or frustrating. Some of them describe ways of working that have proved successful for me or for others I have known. Many of the stories are open-ended accounts of people dealing with problems that come up again and again.

Many are fragments from people's life stories. Nearly everyone I spoke to sees what they are doing now as the result of a series of influences, experiences and emotions that began in childhood. Once we start to talk, it is difficult to shut us up. As spare room tycoons we seem prone to describe our lives as a quest in which we are the heroes. And setbacks are, we hope, only temporary. They steel us and prepare us for the final triumph.

All of these stories contain a lesson, some of them lessons that their tellers know they have to keep learning again and again. Some of the lessons are negative, and others seem to contradict each other. After all, what works for me might not work for you. But I do expect that in most stories you will find a situation or an emotion with which you can identify, and which will assist you in the invention of that one-of-a-kind creation that is your career.

How to be

Being independent is not a task that can ever be completed; it is a way of living. What I would like to do is give my fellow spare room tycoons, and those who are considering joining us, a chance to reflect on their own experiences, problems and approaches by hearing from others who have faced the same challenges.

Spare Room Tycoon is not just a how-to-succeed book, or a how-to-do book. It is more a how-to-be book. When you have only yourself to depend on, you need to make the best use of every resource at your disposal. Many of these resources are intangible things like psychic energy, a sense of self-worth, a belief in spiritual values. Yet, in concentrating on these "softer" aspects of self-employ-ment, I take a very pragmatic view. As an independent business person, you are your most important tool, your most valuable capital, your ultimate resource. If you want your business to survive, you need to understand your-self. Your livelihood—and your sanity—depend on it.

The rewards of self-employment are primarily psy-chical, and the crises are mainly psychological. Anyone can figure out, sooner or later, how to do a balance sheet or create a business plan. What is really hard is keeping going day after day without losing heart, asking to be paid as much as you're worth, and even admitting to yourself that you're happy doing what you do. When I hear my counterparts tell their stories, and when I relate my own, it helps me understand what I'm doing and face the daily challenges of being on my own.

I am not posing as an expert. Think of me more as a friend who has gathered some stories from my own career and from those of others. I am sharing some hard-won experience that I hope will prove useful to you. The people who tell these tales are sharing the secrets of their success. But for most, success is defined not so much by our bank accounts as by the energy and enthusiasm we bring to our work each day and the satisfaction we derive from it. We all see these tales as fragments of larger sto-ries, the adventures of our lives that promise many thrills, heartbreaks and triumphs yet to come.

1
The Way of the Spare Room Tycoon

Being a spare room tycoon is more than just a way of making a living, it is a way of living your life.

It isn't an easy way to live. In the past, being in business independently was the norm, and people typically worked and lived in the same place. That isn't the case today, when most people are employees. Everyone from the tax collector to our mothers would understand us better if we would just go out and get a job.

Moreover, many of us who choose independence make the further decision to stay small. This contradicts a popular conception of entrepreneurship, which holds that everyone wants to run a big business and get rich. If you want to be a spare room tycoon, then, get ready to be misunderstood.

When I talk about spare room tycoons, I often find myself describing what we *aren't*. We aren't unemployed. We aren't between jobs. We don't loll around all day in our pajamas. We aren't failing just because we're not taking on new employees and tripling our business each year. We aren't idle just because we're home, nor, by contrast, are we workaholics just because our home lives and our productive lives frequently overlap.

It is more difficult, given that spare room tycoons are so disparate and represent so many different, strongly held views, to make a positive statement of what we *are*.

My interviewing convinces me, however, that we do have some important common characteristics. One is that we are impatient. We want to do what we want to do when we want to do it, without waiting for someone else to give us permission. And while anxieties and insecurities are our frequent companions, we have a very high estimation of our own abilities. We're people who don't exactly fit in, and are proud not to. We may make our own mistakes sometimes, but we despise making somebody else's. Most of us recall, even as children, having an independent streak and all the troubles and rewards that such a personality can bring. And while I haven't found any research that backs this up, many of us come from families with members who were in business for themselves.

What are we looking for is money, naturally, but we shouldn't be too quick to accept that as the only answer. For all the people in this book, business is more than making money. It is how they express themselves in the world. They can't say that what they do is just a job— because it is not just a job.

What we are looking for, I think, is integrity. We are seeking to integrate all our interests, talents, personality, and character into a way of life that expresses who we are. Of course, we need to compromise; we can't expect always to be doing what we love. Striving for balance in our lives is a never-ending challenge. Most of us discover that we must establish clear boundaries between our personal lives and our careers in order to preserve our health, our families, and our sanity. Nevertheless, even those who draw that line most distinctly still view their businesses as embodiments of their personal talents and values.

It is true that there are also many employees who hope that their work will utilize their talents and enable them to have a lasting and positive impact on the world. (Some such people are strong candidates to become spare room tycoons.) In general, though, our culture doesn't support such aspirations. We are encouraged to view our paycheck as full recompense for our labors, while personal satisfaction is to be found in our private lives, which will be made more elaborate, exciting and fulfilling by all that money can buy.

During an airplane flight when I was first starting work on this book, I read an article in a business magazine. It argued that seeing your business as an outgrowth of yourself is a sickness. The article said that we should view our businesses solely as ways to make a lot of money as quickly as we can. Then we should use that money to live the lives we want. For some this might be relaxation on a small tropical island, but it could also mean writing a novel, engaging in philanthropy, living a life of prayer and contemplation, or playing the stock market.

This argument is attractive because it identifies entrepreneurship with the core beliefs of our society about getting and spending. Moreover, it feeds into our fantasies of riches and freedom. It implies that fabulous wealth is lying around for the taking, available to all. I know I'd love to have enough money to realize all my dreams, and so would the rest of the people in this book. But I also understand enough about the culture I live in to know that I would then begin to have more expensive dreams, and that I'd have to keep laboring to realize those. I'd never be able to disentangle the price of my material indulgences from my value as a person.

Our lives consist not just in how we spend our money but also, and probably more crucially, in what we do to earn it. Our work is the way in which we have an impact on our place and our times. We express ourselves in the world through our work. You can't simply avert your eyes from what you do and still be the sort of person you want to be. You can't just buy a good life. You have to *live* a good life. And though many of us might shy away from such grand pronouncements, living a good life is what most spare room tycoons are trying to do.

How do you do it?

The obvious answer is that we each have to do it in our own way. After all, fierce individualism is the main thing we spare room tycoons have in common. There are probably as many approaches to running one's own business as there are headstrong individuals who want to do so. I have been surprised over and over again as I have researched this book by all the different paths and theories that spare room tycoons follow. Each of these works—at least for the person telling the story—if not necessarily for you or me. It would be foolhardy for me to presume to reduce all this productive idiosyncrasy to a single recipe.

And yet I can imagine you, the readers, shouting back at me: "You've done all these interviews. You've done all this thinking. Haven't you learned anything?"

Of course I have. But what I've discovered is not so much a formula for being in business independently as a framework for thinking about it. This framework might seem most useful for those who are beginning to consider going into business, or who are just starting out. But even those of us who have been out on our own for decades find that we must periodically redefine and recommit to what we do. We need to keep changing what we do, both to assure our survival and to keep from boring ourselves to death. Periodically reexamining the basic premises that underlie our businesses is, I believe, a useful exercise for all.

In order to make the way of the spare room tycoon easier to remember, I've called it SPARE—because its steps are Self-knowledge, Passion, Action, Realization and Evolution. Let's look at each of these in turn.

Self-knowledge

Self-knowledge is an analytical process: a clear-eyed, hard-headed look at one's own capabilities, inclinations, and behavior. It is the opposite of self-indulgence. Self-knowledge is not easy to attain.

Why start with something so hard? My answer is that it is almost the only place you can start. Not unless you ask yourself some difficult questions can you begin to determine whether you're suited to becoming a spare room tycoon.

Many people think about going into business on their own when their work situation becomes intolerable. It's important to consider, however, whether you are having a problem with your particular employer and your particular boss, or whether your problem is with virtually all employers and all bosses.

If the latter is true, you are probably on your way to self-employment. Many of those I interviewed recognized that they had experienced difficulties with authority their entire lives. They felt that being in business for themselves was probably their only sensible option. And on days when things go wrong, they said, their greatest consolation is their own independence.

Many who forsake the life of the employee don't realize all they are going to lose, far more than the fringe benefits and the luxury and security of paid vacations. Work environments are sociable places. You become accustomed to hearing the latest gossip, keeping up with the newest jokes, seeing what other people are wearing. You make friends and enemies, all of which make life interesting. Besides, working as part of a team can be an intensely satisfying experience. Large organizations are able to get big things done. You might be frustrated by the internal politics that seem to stand in your way, but you need to think seriously about whether you will be able to start from zero, with only yourself to depend on.

Having a regular job gives life a sense of structure that we independents must struggle to recreate. You should ask yourself whether you can muster the discipline to deploy your energies in a systematic way when there's nobody—except perhaps your creditors—expecting you to do anything. Your success in creating a busi-

ness can depend as much on your seriousness and professionalism as on the strength of your ideas. This is
something you can learn, obviously, but you should
nevertheless think about whether it is something that
comes naturally to you.

I have also found that even people who consider
themselves to be dissatisfied employees rely very
strongly on their jobs for a sense of identity. It gives them
a place in their communities. It gives them an arena
where they exercise power that others recognize. If nothing else, it allows them to answer the question "What do
you do?" without feeling twinges of insecurity.

The issues I have proposed thus far have mostly
dealt with whether you have the personality to make it on
your own. It is equally important, however, to think about
your skills, interests and knowledge that can contribute
to your business's uniqueness and success.

Most people begin their businesses as a logical step
from the job they were doing before. Your job provides
knowledge of an industry—its economics, its procedures,
its technologies, its problems. All of these can provide
clues to help you determine the services or products you
can profitably provide.

But, in most cases, the most important thing you
know from your previous work is people. A few might be
potential customers, suppliers or clients. Others can be
sources of information. It is much easier to make sensible
decisions if you are part of a network in a particular field.
As an outsider, it takes a while to learn enough to become
accepted and to take advantage of the opportunities that
being part of the industry can offer. Such people are also
useful as sounding boards. It is very beneficial to try your

ideas out on smart, informed people before you rush into them. They might point out opportunities or problems that you didn't see.

At the same time, it is equally important not to let the sensible practice of basing your new career on your current one blind you to strengths and interests you may not have been exploiting in your previous employment.

Once, during a crisis in my own career, I decided to make an inventory of my interests and abilities. The work I was doing fit into a goal I had developed long ago of bringing Chinese and western cultures closer together. Still, I was not happy with what I was doing day in and day out. It was important for me to distinguish that rather lofty and abstract goal from the things I was actually doing. I wanted to know what I do well, what I enjoy doing, and what I would like to learn more about.

I wrote down some things that had always been part of my practice and my life, though I had never thought of them as central. Among these were being in front of the public, speaking and giving seminars. And there were a few things on the list that I had done only for myself, such as writing. Yet once I had recorded these desires, they became part of what I wanted to become. You are reading one of the results.

The crisis passed and my business improved, but it became subtly different. Giving seminars became a distinct part of my practice. Awareness of my desire to work in this area led me to learn techniques for training people effectively in business settings. An interest became a strength, and eventually an income stream. But it began with an inventory of my strengths, interests and desires.

In short, self-knowledge means that you know who you are and that you want to transform who you are into a business. But merely having self-knowledge is not enough to give you the fuel to transform yourself. To do this, you must have passion.

Passion

When I say passion, I don't mean just your innate talents, skills, experiences, contacts, abilities and all those things that, once you've completed the above self-exercise with self-knowledge, you know you have. You can't quantify passion, enumerate it, put it on a chart. Passion is a wild card; it transforms and gives power to all the rest.

It is difficult to look for passion directly. It's like the sun—you see it obliquely and you feel its heat. There are some sorts of passion you can scarcely avoid. Needing to be on your own is just such a passion for many people. You can find other passions by spying on yourself and surreptitiously noting the things you do without thinking much about them.

Have you ever gotten involved in doing something and become so engrossed that you've forgotten that you're doing the work? That's passion. If you have to ask over and over again why you're doing what you're doing, you have no passion in your work.

The most celebrated recent example of a passion that became a big business concerns a woman who was devoted to collecting Pez dispensers, little plastic containers for hard candy. Collectors are often quietly passionate people, who delight in the thrill of the hunt for the perfect, elusive object that will make their collection more compelling. This woman convinced her husband to create a site on the internet so that Pez collectors could find each other and trade their wares. It quickly became apparent that such a site could be about more than candy containers. It could be a business, and a big one. It's called eBay, one of the biggest success stories of the World Wide Web. It even makes money.

Unquestionably, there was much more involved in creating this valuable business than a passion for Pez. But a private passion is what got the whole thing started. The company wouldn't exist without it.

Passion is what makes the spare room tycoon come up with new ideas and new ways of doing things. Passion enables spare room tycoons to be competitive. Because we are doing what we love to do, we are harder to beat than people who are in it only for the money. Customers and clients sense our passion. They may not want to become like us. But when they need assistance in an area where we are equipped to help, they know they want us because we are at peace with what we do. Clients can be confident that they are have found the right people to provide what they need.

Once you gain knowledge about who you are and what you're passionate about, you'll be ready to take the next step: action.

Action

Many people who work in companies fantasize about going into business for themselves. But they only think about it. They're not serious about it. It is not enough to know who you are and what your passions are. You must make a leap in order to discover whether your talents and passions can really make a business.

Making this leap—forgoing your paycheck and embarking on what seems like an endless journey into the unknown—is exhilarating and often terrifying. But many people have done it. And you'll never know what you can do until you try.

What I have learned by interviewing successful spare room tycoons is that different people have different ways of making the leap to independence. Some are convinced that you must do extensive preparation before quitting your job. They say that you must at least research the market, identify potential clients, write a business plan that will both work for you and convince potential lenders and investors. Ideally, you should also get the business going, at least part-time, in order to test whether your ideas will work.

I did some of that. I printed my stationery, bought my power suits, and sent out what proved to be a very effective promotion letter. Before I left my job, I had several solid prospects. Still, I didn't spend too much time wondering if and when I should begin.

Others set up their businesses with less preparation. Some of them practically got up in the morning and found themselves in business. All they had was a telephone, a pencil, a notebook and a Rolodex. Emotionally, their new life had begun.

Whether we plan for it or plunge into it, we can't succeed if we don't take action.

Of course, you might also fail. Many small businesses do, though the figures are contradictory and not very reliable. One frequently quoted source says that over half of small businesses fail within the first three years and only about 15 percent will still be in business after ten years. These numbers may be misleading, because they mix different kinds of businesses with different life expectancies. Sometimes even very successful restaurants, for example, don't make it to their tenth anniversary.

The real reason not to be preoccupied with this seemingly bleak statistic is that it does not measure another kind of failure—the failure to try. Who knows how many stillborn businesses there are, possibly very successful ones, that were doomed by a loss of nerve, an unwillingness finally to take action.

People succeed because they go ahead and try. No matter how much we attempt to prepare for making the break into independence, taking that final step requires bravery.

And surviving that step is the beginning of confidence. We see that we can make business happen on our own. We build our confidence like a muscle, by facing anxieties, meeting challenges, and discovering that we have lived to tell the tale.

As I interviewed other spare room tycoons, I found out that I was not the only person who jumped up and down in ecstasy when my business got its first chunk of income. Just about all of us exult, each in our own way, when faced with the miracle of someone willing to pay for what we offer. These first customers don't mean our troubles are over, merely that we have dived into business and discovered that we can float. Now it's time to swim.

Realization

Realization is a double-edged idea.

We want to think that it means that our vision has become a reality, that our aspirations are being fulfilled. It is also associated with self-realization, the hope that we have become what we really are meant to be.

Neither of these ideas is wrong. They are what keep us going. Somehow or other, most spare room tycoons want to change the world. We measure our success not only by our net financial worth but by our impact on those around us.

But before this higher realization takes place, there are realizations of a different sort. We realize that our business plan was faulty. We realize that the marketing approach we have adopted is falling on deaf ears. We realize, perhaps, that those we were counting on to be customers aren't willing to pay for what we offer. But we may also realize that there are other potential customers we never anticipated and other things we can provide that buyers really want.

Sometimes it seems that the more we prepare, the harder reality hits us in the face. That's because it's possible to become too self-absorbed and create a business plan that is too rigid. Those who are more natural risk takers realize that they must learn from whatever the real world throws at them. But those who feel most certain that they have everything figured out are at the greatest risk of a premature sense of failure.

Starting a business is an encounter with forces far more powerful than yourself. Among these are the economy, both local and global. Few businesses are so small that they are immune from events happening halfway around the world. Many of us are also affected by political actions, which range from regulations and government contracts to the sort of explosive event like that in Beijing's Tiananmen Square in 1989 that, for a time, decimated my China consulting practice, as we will see later. Technology continually offers new opportunities, while speeding up the pace of change. And cultural phenomena—from fashions in clothes and home furnishings and how and what people eat, to family size and educational expectations—may be the most powerful forces of all. They bring new businesses into being all the time, while destroying others that fail to adapt.

To be one man or one woman engaging these powerful forces is what gives being in business on your own so much excitement and fear. It's no accident that one of those interviewed in the book says he gave up competitive hang-gliding, rock climbing and scuba diving when he went into business for himself. Being a spare room tycoon is adventure enough.

People often speak of starting a small business as if it were like building a house. The structure is static. The forces that might knock it down are more or less predictable. A better metaphor might be climbing a mountain or surfing, activities that require extensive preparation and demand expertise, but can nevertheless be counted on to surprise even the most experienced practitioner.

The key skill we must cultivate during this realization stage is being open to what the world is telling us. When a prospect turns you down, you must pay very close attention to what she is saying, even after she says no. When something you see as a small part of your business does very well, you need to ask why, and think about what that implies for the business as a whole. When a competitor whose offerings you feel are inferior to yours repeatedly beats you, you need to consider not only what you are doing wrong, but also what the competitor is doing right.

Realization is the fun part of business, though it doesn't always seem so. If you were able to take an idea and bring it effortlessly to reality, it would quickly become boring. You would be like a child with a shiny toy that is locked in a box. If you can't play with it, there's no point to it.

The great thing about a business is that you keep learning about it. You keep seeing it from different angles. You never stop learning. You're surprised by what you've done wrong, and by what you've done right. Running your business builds confidence and humility—both at the same time.

Evolution

Initial success is easier to achieve than many would want to admit. It is what you must do *after* that first success that is difficult—changing yourself when it is time to do so.

All businesses have to adapt to circumstances in order to survive and prosper. Even multinational companies disappear if they don't evolve, let alone personal businesses like ours. No matter how fervent our personal or business goals are, we need to be reconsidering and adapting them continually. That way we can meet the needs of the marketplace, and satisfy our own changing desires as well.

When I first started my business, I was single-mindedly devoted to achieving a romantic goal, namely, to pull China and America closer together while making a living doing it. I would not, and could not, imagine doing anything else. I equated romantic devotion with personal authenticity. Then the Tiananmen Square incident took place. China and America were not keen to do business with each other for a while. My personal myth had helped me clarify my goals. My passion had given me the fire to keep going. But all this became irrelevant in the face of geopolitical events that, I reluctantly admitted, had absolutely nothing to do with me.

Yet I was nevertheless challenged to find out what I should be doing in the face of such a change. I returned to the beginning of the SPARE process by engaging in self-examination of my skills and talents, to see how they could be redeployed in an altered environment. I also searched for my passions, and found myself reaching back to a previously abandoned career I thought I had hated, college teaching. I realized that I had loved the teaching; it was the college I hated. I also broadened my geographic reach. And, though I resisted this until I had little choice, I took a stopgap job that actually strengthened both my skills and my credentials when I was able to return to being a spare room tycoon.

Learning from my own experience and from the experience of other people who are even more successful than I am, I've now taught myself to think strategically, not just romantically. While I treasure my own personal myth and would never want to let go of it, I have been telling myself these past few years that I must look at the world and not just China or even Asia. I must read the daily papers, see the evening news, mingle with people, watch what is going on in the world. My objective is to find something that might provide the clue for the next stage of my business.

If you feel that your business has grown to a stage where you can't see a significant breakthrough, it is time to think about what you can do next to diversify or to change your approach. If the phone rings and suddenly someone is asking you—and paying you—to do something that you can do but never quite thought about doing, don't say no. I would highly recommend that you do it. Good things don't just fall into your lap for no good reason. Fortune may be telling you that you are the right person in the right place at the right time. That's the best luck of all.

What is most important about evolution, however, is that it provides a better way than sheer growth to judge the development of a business. Biological evolution consists of successful adaptation to ever-changing circumstances. The environment offers countless biological niches, and all sorts of creatures have evolved to flourish within them. Some adaptations create new niches of their own. Large creatures, like the whale, the mammoth or the dinosaurs, have evolved at different times. But these are not the only "successes" of evolution, nor are small creatures examples of evolution's failure. There are all sorts of right sizes for animals, and there are also all sorts of right sizes for businesses.

The biological metaphor can't be pushed too far, however. Evolution in nature proceeds by chance. The evolution of our business depends entirely on our responsiveness, creativity, and energy. We cannot decree or design what we will become, but we do shape it by how well we respond to the challenges we face.

Such uncertainty leads to worry. But after you have been in business for a while, you realize that it is also the chief source of hope. No matter what you are today, you can become something more, something different tomorrow. Our businesses evolve because both the market demands that they must and we spare room tycoons desire that they do.

Evolution seems to be the final stage of the SPARE model, but it also leads right back to the beginning: Self-knowledge. You can't really know where to go next without re-examining who you are. Then you'll need to get back in touch with your passions, and plan a course of action.

The five elements of SPARE—Self-knowledge, Passion, Action, Realization and Evolution—work like five strokes of an unending cycle of activity that drives the spare room tycoon.

In the chapters that follow, I will recount real-life stories from my own experience and that of three dozen others that show how we have juggled these components of SPARE and found success—in our distinctly individual ways.

Starting

2
Knowing What to Do

As a spare room tycoon, you are your business's chief asset. Your future livelihood, and that of those who count on you, will depend on your skills, your knowledge, and your ability to perform.

That's a scary thought, one that most of us would rather not face directly. That's why many of us devote more effort and energy to evaluating the quality and durability of a new car, computer or piece of furniture than we do to considering how well we're going to hold up over the long haul.

Besides, going into business independently isn't always something we can plan for long in advance. As you will see in the first story in this chapter, I made the leap somewhat impulsively, and so did many of the people with whom I spoke.

Nevertheless, even those who don't have the time or the inclination to conduct due diligence about themselves find, sooner rather than later, that disciplined introspection is a valuable tool. It helps them to understand not just what they want to do, but also what they do so well that others are willing to pay them for it.

Nearly everyone I interviewed for this book offered a life story that resulted, through determination or fate, in what they are doing right now. Often these tales tell of youthful frustration and other paths taken before spare room tycoons finds themselves, decades later, fulfilling these earlier ambitions, albeit in unexpected ways. These life stories we tell ourselves are, I believe, very important. They are myths that inform us where to start, help us to succeed, and enable us to sustain ourselves and see the inevitable evolution of our lives as progress, rather than failure. It's nevertheless important that we tell ourselves the right life stories, those that really reflect our achievements and desires. The wrong life story can lead to bad moves in the future.

Just by becoming a spare room tycoon, and taking on challenges you have never faced before, you will learn a great deal about yourself. The key is to pay attention.

Declaration of independence

The climax to my own story of becoming a spare room tycoon took place in a parking lot in a restaurant near Disney World in Florida. That's where I decided, seemingly on impulse, to leave my job and go into business independently. Yet I had the feeling then, as I do now, that this apparently rash and unexpected act was one for which I had long been preparing. It was a moment when the shape of my life was suddenly clearer than it had been before.

Going independent is a leap into the unknown. It is striking to me how many spare room tycoons recall this leap not so much as an act of bold risk taking, but rather as a moment when they suddenly understood something about themselves. This insight provides the confidence to jump into the risky, often rewarding, life of the independent.

Here's my story: I was a manager at a subsidiary of a large company that was about to move from Manhattan to Florida. I wasn't sure I wanted to make the move. I was working for a vice-president who hadn't wanted to hire me, and didn't hesitate to let me know that. The man who had hired me originally was heading up the Canadian division and couldn't offer much help. I felt it would be far worse to be fired or forced out of the company once I had uprooted myself and was away from my friends and contacts. Besides, I had a friend I didn't want to leave.

Nevertheless, I accepted the company's offer of a one-week, all-expenses-paid trip to Orlando. For the first six days I wandered in Disney World, and drove around pondering whether to trade the mean streets of New York for a humid, alligator-fringed suburb. I even went to a park and looked at some alligators. The big city felt far friendlier.

Then I thought about continuing to work with people I held in contempt, and who didn't like me much either. I wanted to tell myself that I should be a good company boy; I was much younger then. I must learn to be a good soldier. And one day I might even become vice-president. I didn't like that future, but I couldn't see an alternative. Despite all I was feeling, I was ready by the end of my one-week sojourn to say yes to the company and accept their offer for me to work in Florida.

Night came. I felt restless in the motel room. I hopped into the car and drove aimlessly. Then I saw the large, green road sign pointing toward Disney Village. I followed it. All was dark. The only light I saw was a restaurant, quite an expensive one, in Disney Village. I got out of the car, looked at the menu and said to myself, "Wouldn't it be nice to eat at expensive restaurants and not have to worry about the price?"

Immediately I realized how impoverished this fantasy was. I was going to move to a place I didn't like to work for a boss I didn't respect, devoting my energies to office politics for which I had little talent. I would make all of this sacrifice so that I could afford the surf and turf at an elaborately mediocre restaurant on the outskirts of nowhere. I was going to continue to do something I didn't want to do so that I could afford things I didn't want very much either. This was my life, and I was getting set to waste it.

I decided instead to take control of that life, to start a business, to live where I like, and to change the world. I didn't even think about looking for another job. That would just be moving to another part of the swamp. Never again did I want to place my career at the mercy of a fool. I would become a self-employed, independent consultant. The only fool I'd be beholden to would be myself.

I got back in my car and drove to my motel. I called my friend and announced that I was going to quit my job and become an independent consultant. That was my original scene. I made the leap of faith by the restaurant glow, alone in the dark Disney Village. I've never looked back. I've never regretted leaving the corporate life.

It has been 17 years since that night. I am free. I feel free. I own myself. I don't feel that any one person can tell me that he or she feeds me; I feed myself. This is what I want. And this is what I am.

Identifying your strengths

Some people, like me, recall the main turning points of their lives and careers as coming in instantaneous flashes of insight that changed everything. For many others, in contrast, there is no moment of suddenly realizing what they were meant to do. Finding their path is deliberative, not impulsive, and it can take months or years to happen.

Marilyn Bellock has invented a unique career for herself, one that is perfectly attuned both to her interests and to contemporary business trends. She works primarily for European fashion, design and home furnishings companies to develop new products, primarily for the American market. These are companies with famous, high-quality brands that Marilyn finds ways to extend into new product areas while still retaining the cachet that gives them value.

"My friends all tell me that I'm so lucky to be doing what I'm doing," Marilyn says. And she admits that it is, in many ways, the ideal job for her. It combines her interest in fashion and design, the nose for news she developed in her earlier journalistic career, and the financial and business planning expertise she developed by getting an MBA and working for a large media company. But, as she sees it, luck had little to do with it. Her career seems tailor-made for her because she was the tailor, and she worked hard at making it fit.

Marilyn held a responsible position with a large salary. She appeared very successful, but inwardly she struggled and brooded about what she really ought to be doing. She suspected that her greatest strength is that she combines aesthetic and imaginative dimensions with a sound, clear business sense. "I'm a hybrid," she says. "In a corporate environment, I'm creative. And if I'm in a creative environment, I'm very corporate." This insight gave her a clue, but hardly an answer to her quandary. She knew that her ambition was not to climb the management ladder, but to devise a career in which she would answer to herself. She was becoming impatient. "Time was going past, but where was I?" Marilyn says. "What would be the next, best thing?"

Her corporate job involved making business plans for the company. These can be complex, but their goal is almost always quite clear: to make more profits. Marilyn wanted money, too, but she found that making plans for herself was much more difficult, because she was seeking personal satisfaction and self-realization along with financial rewards.

Even after a year of trying, Marilyn couldn't come up with a plan for her own career. Furious at herself, she developed a regimen to discipline her thinking about her ultimate goals.

The first thing she decided was to set aside time each day to think about what she wanted to do. She stopped going to work by subway and started to walk. Previously, her commute had been simply about getting to work. But now her walk to work was a distinct part of the day, one that belonged to her and not to her job.

At the end of each day, Marilyn made a list of the thoughts that came to her while walking to and from work, and in other private moments of reflection. Periodically, she would go back to these notes and see what patterns might be emerging.

She also began to keep track of her routine behavior, the things that she did not for work, or consciously for recreation, but simply out of habit. This made her conscious of the number of design and home furnishing magazines she purchased and perused throughout the week. She realized that she had not only a deep interest in these products and industries, but a substantial amount of knowledge as well.

Armed with this information about herself, she began to think about how design- and fashion-driven companies are managed. As she walked to work, she reflected that many extremely creative people have difficulty with her kind of systematic, strategic thinking. Morning after morning, between dodging panhandlers and bouts of window shopping, a vision began to emerge.

She decided to target European home furnishings companies to help them develop new lines of products. She quickly discovered that when she told the executives of these companies that they could open whole new revenue streams, they were almost always willing to hear what she had to say. She started her business in 1990, and now works for many of the biggest names in European design and fashion.

Marilyn counsels others to have big, long-term plans, something she believes women have a particular problem with because they get bogged down in the details of family life. She sees no contradiction between this advice and her own experience, which depended on teasing out the details of her habits and desires to determine what she ought to do.

"You must take time to find out what you want," says Marilyn. "There are at least five reasons for everything that happens in life. I always find out what these reasons are and assess their consequences."

From passion to product

When going into business for yourself, it is very helpful to have appropriate training, experience in your industry, and the contacts who can help get you going. But one factor that is often overlooked may really be the most important: a passionate commitment to what you are doing. And the spark for a successful business is just as likely to come from your personal life as from your professional one.

Denise Devine says that she never aspired to start her own business. She was trained as a certified public accountant, and her career had been spent in large accounting firms and in huge corporations. "I never thought of myself as an entrepreneur," she says. "I never thought of myself as a risk taker." She did wonder, however, whether a woman could advance much farther up the hierarchy of the multinational food processing company for which she worked.

What set her off in a new direction was concern over her two-year-old, Nick, who loved to drink fruit juices and carbonated soft drinks all day. She began to look critically at what he was ingesting, and realized that the products consisted mostly of sugar. She worried that he preferred these sweet drinks to food that could provide him with calcium and other minerals and vitamins that he needed.

At about the same time, the US Department of Agriculture released nutritional guidelines recommending that people eat six to eleven servings of grains per day and five servings of vegetables and fruits.

Denise recalled thinking about how people could find foods that would help them follow these guidelines, without forcing them to spend far more time each day preparing foods. She also felt that her employer was missing an opportunity by failing to produce the foods that would enable consumers to follow a healthy diet. She asked herself whether the nutrition Nick needed could be engineered into a product that Nick would drink.

She was able to get some initial money from a government-financed venture capital fund, and eventually she found a food chemist at Cornell University who was willing to try. The technology they developed involves processing whole grains such as oats, barley and rice into a smooth liquid containing all their fiber and nutrients. Once it's flavored with fruit, it becomes Devine Nectar, a relatively painless and kid-friendly start to a nutritious diet. The same technology can also be used for ice cream, puddings, sauces and other kinds of products.

"I want to capitalize on my creativity," Denise says. "Big companies reward people for not making mistakes. The idea of making juices from grains is new, but I see it as the opportunity of a lifetime." Her background in finance has helped her line up investors she believes will be sufficiently patient to see the technology perfected and marketed effectively.

Nick, the child who started it all, is 11 now, and his mother reports that at least some of the time he drinks Devine Nectar, which is currently in limited commercial distribution.

Devine Foods Inc. is a virtual company. The research and development is contracted out, as is the manufacturing. Denise is also exploring joint ventures to produce new products, among them a milkshake with low sugar, high calcium and fiber. "How can a CPA be the co-inventor of three chemical composition patents?" she asks. The answer is, of course, that she had the idea. Her passion is what made the technology happen.

"This is not something I have a choice in," says Denise of what she calls "the emotional rollercoaster" of self-employment. "This is something I feel compelled to do. This is what I was meant to do."

Reclaiming a dream

Finding the right path can often involve a series of false starts and dramatic changes of direction. Yet in retrospect, you discover that you have done exactly what was needed to find the right way to go. That was exactly what happened to Ruth Dalphin, who took a circuitous route toward what she had wanted to do as a girl.

When she was young, she dreamed of going to medical school. She was fascinated by the way people's minds work, and she wanted to study psychiatry. But her family discouraged her from medical school, saying they couldn't afford it. So she followed her other passion: music. She became an excellent bassoonist and won a scholarship to a prestigious music school. After she graduated, she immediately began teaching at the University of Delaware and playing professionally.

She enjoyed her music, but she also found it enormously stressful. The bassoon is a technically demanding instrument. Besides, giving recitals or playing solos on any instrument induces anxiety, while playing as part of an orchestra represents the opposite of the independence that Ruth has sought all her life.

In order to deal with this stress, she began to take lessons in meditation and practicing it. Before long, she started work with some of her music students on breathing exercises and relaxation techniques. She also became interested in naturopathic medicine, combining the study of body, mind, spirit, food, and exercise. She took some math classes with the idea of going back to school to study science. "I kept seeing myself wanting to do something other than playing the bassoon, but not knowing what," Ruth recalls.

The answer came one day while she was meditating. She saw herself in front of a large audience dressed entirely in white, in contrast with the black costume she wore when performing as a musician. As she thought about this vision, it occurred to her that rather than teach music, she might teach meditation. She began to advertise a six-week course on meditation and health, and got going by persuading friends and fellow musicians to sign up.

For Ruth, an instinctive achiever, meditation was not a way to drop out of the world, but rather to become more fully involved. She began to study Shiatsu massage and yoga. She eventually married one of her teachers of Shiatsu, Judah Roseman, and the two started their own business teaching Asian healing arts. Ruth stopped teaching bassoon.

The seriousness and rigor with which they studied their disciplines made them stand out during the mid-1980s, and they traveled throughout the US to teach and to Asia to study. Their school won certification from the state of New Jersey and they opened Associates for Creative Wellness to help people deal with health problems.

Judah died a few years ago. "The business is our only baby," Ruth says. She has one full-time employee and a dozen contractors working for her now.

"I've never intended to be very wealthy," she comments. "My wealthy clients say to me, 'My children are unruly, my husband is screaming. What should I do?' They own multimillion-dollar houses, and they come to me to tell them how to live."

Ruth's answers for life are much the same as she has found in her business. "Discover who you are, what gives you energy, what makes you happy," she says. "Find people you want to be with. Do more of the things that make you happy and fulfilled. You can build a better business if you can identify your strengths and build on them. See what has to be done and find people who can do the job. Then give your vision feet and wings."

Moment of commitment

Unlike most of the people in this book, Aram Fox had never dreamed of being in business independently. Indeed, he had made many of the key decisions of his life so that he would live completely differently from his parents, who ran their own business. And until a crucial moment, he told himself a story that made him oblivious to his own strengths and deep desires.

Aram can pinpoint his decision to go into business for himself almost to the minute. It was some time between 9.30 and 10 am, Frankfurt time, on a Sunday morning in October. He was tired from jet lag, and slightly hung over from having had too much to drink the night before. He was walking across a sprawling exhibition floor at the Frankfurt Book Fair, on his way to an appointment with a German publisher who was interested in helping him set up a business. His intention was to say no.

As the child of a family business, he knew far too much about the travails of self-employment. From the time he was a boy, he noticed that his parents, partners in a jewelry manufacturing business, worked incessantly, worried about the business when they weren't working, and had little choice but to shoulder large financial risks without the likelihood of large profits.

Aram's determination not to follow in his parents' footsteps took him first to the University of Chicago, where he studied literary theory. Despite his good grades and intellectual seriousness, he found himself drawn in more practical and entrepreneurial directions. An unpaid internship with a film company led to barely paid assignments as a script reader. He was, in fact, self-employed, but he didn't view this as a career choice, merely as a way to survive while trying to write a novel. He did enjoy making his own hours, dressing as he pleased, and taking afternoon walks in Central Park.

After a couple of years of this he took a temporary job with a big publisher that turned into a permanent, more responsible job. He decided to quit when his boss, whom he admired, left in order to write a novel of his own. Aram found work at a literary agency where, for the first time, he felt he was doing just what he wanted to. His experience in movies and publishing made him ideally suited to the role of scout, the sort of person who knows what books are being written and which movie producers and foreign publishers might be interested in the product.

The publisher Aram was going to see that morning in Frankfurt obviously believed that he was talented. Three times he had urged Aram to break away from the agency he worked for and set up his own firm, to which the publisher promised support and business. Three times Aram, flashing back to his parents and their labors, had said no. Aram feared that the publisher would broach the topic again in their face-to-face meeting. But he couldn't avoid it because the publisher was simply too important a business contact.

He figured that it would take him 20 minutes to cross the chaotic, congested hall. The journey was every bit as slow and unpleasant as he had anticipated, but as he made his way through the hordes, Aram felt his grumpiness give way to insight. He recalled that, while he didn't want to become his parents, his own period of self-employment had been very pleasant. Moreover, it occurred to him that just about all the unhappiness and frustration he felt in his role as a literary scout were produced by the agency he worked for, not by the job itself. "And everything I did like about scouting," he recalls thinking, "I would like more if I were running my own company."

By 10 o'clock, when he reached the publisher's booth, the heaviness of half an hour before had dissipated and was replaced by a feeling of freedom. The publisher began the meeting by asking Aram his opinion of a particular title. Aram spoke freely, then disagreed with some aspects of what the publisher said. The publisher didn't seem disturbed by the disagreements. Indeed, he seemed to respect Aram more. This was a crucial test of freedom and respect. So when the publisher asked once again if Aram would consider setting up a new firm, Aram said yes.

Aram is young, 26 when we talked, and his firm was only a few months old, but prospering. "I've never been this happy," he says. Then he adds something that explains both his choice of career and the way that he thinks about it: "I love drama."

❖❖❖

Deciding to become independent is probably the single most important business decision you will make. It is also a decision about your life. Like love, it sometimes feels as if you're just falling into it.

Nevertheless, there usually turns out to be not just one but several reasons to choose the course you follow. For example, a crisis with an employer might hurry your decision along, but once you're in business you discover you're doing something you have been thinking about since childhood. Sometimes a job you hate allows you to develop skills that prove useful to a career you love.

Much depends on the life stories we tell ourselves. Usually, these are explanations after the fact, attempts to make random events make sense. Nevertheless, these stories are important. Telling yourself the wrong stories can lead you to the wrong conclusions and to bad decisions in the future.

No decision about what you ought to do is ever final. You need to keep monitoring your own desires, carry on talking to other people, and pay attention to where the money is. And you have to realize that everyone makes mistakes along the way. Figuring out what you want— and what the world wants—is something you'll need to do for as long as you're in business.

3
Meeting the Market

There is really only one certainty about starting your own business: You really have no idea what it is going to be like.

The beginning of a business can be an exhilarating time. Those first assignments or initial customers affirm that you weren't imagining things when you decided to become independent. It is reassuring, even thrilling, to discover that what you are doing is real and useful, and that people are willing to pay for it. That's what you thought, or at least hoped. Still, it's wonderful to be proven right.

It's also close to inevitable that you will be proven wrong. Some of your ideas will turn out to be too optimistic, a little naïve, or completely erroneous. Many spare room tycoons try out a number of different business models before they hit on the one that works for them. Very few people will be able to get everything right from the outset. Finding out what you have to offer and what people will pay for can never be a one-time event. The world is changing and so are you. You need to be alert to clues about what you might do next.

Reality rarely, if ever, follows our plans. And although we might be tempted to see that as reality's problem, it's really ours. Spare room tycoons need to be agile, fast, wily. Indeed, that's one of the most important advantages we have over large organizations. But because we sometimes isolate ourselves with our own visions, we occasionally don't respond as quickly as we should to what the world is telling us.

That's what starting up is all about. You have to pay attention to what you're doing and learn fast. Some day, you might look back at your mistakes as a beginner and be able to laugh about them. Right now, though, they feel serious, and you feel stupid. You will just have to work your way through them; you haven't any choice.

Starting out is also when you feel the full impact of what you have given up. You know that you will have to do without the security of a weekly salary. It's a different thing to have bills coming in and know that you will have to scramble to pay them this month and every month from now on.

Something else you may not expect is how much you miss the identity your old job gave you. You may no longer have been satisfied with the role you were playing, but at least you *had* a role. Many of us, especially those who held prestigious positions, suddenly feel naked when we are out on our own.

Even more devastating is the subtle evidence of a loss of power. People used to go out of their way to say hello to you. Now they don't bother because you don't have the power you used to have. It can take a long time to learn to live without the place in the world that our old employers lent us.

Eventually, though, you will be able to deal with this. The point of the effort is to escape from assigned roles and shape a career that satisfies you. And you have to start somewhere.

Smelling blood

My own leap into independence depended not only on my moment of self-knowledge at Disney World, but also on an earlier discovery that what I was doing could pay.

In 1979, the US normalized relations with China. I was a college professor teaching at Cortland in pastoral upstate New York. I was overjoyed at the news. I didn't know why I was so jubilant about the normalization. I guess I felt that this event would create opportunities I was not yet able to see. I somehow knew that a "door" had just been opened, for me as well as for China and the US. I could take another journey in my life, away from an academic career with which I was becoming increasingly dissatisfied.

Because I was bilingual, bicultural, with a PhD from a top school, I found work at a large publishing company. Along the way I had discussed jobs with a large bank, an oil company, an air-freight company and a commodities brokerage. Every morning the newspapers printed new stories showing that China was on the verge. Every day, I met people who told me what a lucky position I was in.

They were right. I was able to go through that opening door. I succeeded in helping my company make money in the China market. Sales for China doubled within 18 months. And sales to Southeast Asian countries, which were within my area of responsibility, tripled in the same period. I gained confidence.

One day at work, I got a thin letter from a Chinese importer in the mail. I opened the letter. It was a $150,000 prepayment for some scientific journals that I hadn't been expecting. At that moment, everything seemed to come together: The need was there. The money was there. I had made the right things happen. I smelled blood.

Even at the time, I knew that I hadn't done it all by myself. I was a beneficiary of circumstance, someone who was in the right place at the right time. Soon, in fact, the Chinese started to pirate those same journals and fewer large checks were forthcoming. And the years I have spent as a consultant have not all been euphoric ones for China and Southeast Asia. There have been some very bad times.

But the recollection of receiving that check still energizes me. It was the moment I realized that what I wanted to do in life could actually make a profit. People who want to be in business on their own need to have a similar experience of tripping over money and opportunities. You need to feel the elation of doing something that works.

If things aren't as easy as they first seemed, that's to be expected. But once you've caught the scent and know success is possible, you have the courage to slash your way through the jungle to pursue your quarry.

Is there money in it?

When you are doing what you love, the money doesn't necessarily follow. You have to be doing something that people value highly enough to provide the level of income you require. If what you are doing doesn't produce high enough personal or economic rewards, that's not a judgment of you as a person. It just means you should look for situations where what you have to offer will be more highly rewarded.

Joe Dolan went into business for himself more than 80 years ago, when he was 14 years old. That's when he had put together enough money to acquire a small boat suitable for catching lobsters in the shallow waters near where he grew up on Long Island Sound.

As he recalled years later, he spent the first year or two working very hard and becoming a more skillful lobsterman. Then he had an insight. "I looked at the fellow who was the best in the harbor, and I figured that I'd probably never get any better than him," he said. "Then I looked at how he lived—in a not very nice house with his children wearing patched clothes, and always having to worry about whether he was going to get by."

At that point he decided to become a wholesaler. He kept on putting out his own traps and selling his own lobsters, but he was able to convince his fellow lobstermen that he should sell theirs for them as well. He quickly established a reputation as a shrewd but entirely reliable businessman, and his colleagues were probably better off paying him something to make their deals than they would have been on their own.

Many spare room tycoons start out doing one thing, then shift to something else for which they discover both a talent and a better possibility of material rewards. Joe did this again and again throughout a very complicated career. He eventually became a seafood retailer, a restaurateur, the owner of a small fishing fleet, a banker, a politician and a famous hunting guide—all at the same time! Never in his life did he have to show up at an office and spend a full day there. From the time he started out on his lobster boat at 14, he kept discovering different ways to be his own man.

Keep listening after "no"

Nobody likes to be turned down. Rejection can make you feel as if you want to close your eyes and stop up your ears and simply disappear from the face of the earth.

But many times, just after a prospect has declared he doesn't need what you offer, he'll keep talking. As my friend Rick Schilling found out, paying close attention at such moments can be rewarding. That's how he was able to figure out what companies would really be willing to pay him to do.

Rick had worked for one of the Philadelphia region's largest banks for 19 years. In the late 1980s, when banks throughout the US started swallowing each other and spitting out their loyal employees, Rick and many of his colleagues found themselves self-employed, whether they liked it or not.

Rick had held an important position. He knew a lot about banks, the people who run them, and the people who do business with them. He was certain that he could find a way to put all this knowledge to work.

Nevertheless, he hit several dead ends. His first venture was an equipment leasing business. That went sour quickly. Then he tried consulting with small businesses on how to deal with banks, get loans and manage their credit requirements. His experience as a banker had convinced him that many small companies need such help. He was probably correct, but there was a serious problem: His prospective clients weren't willing to pay for what he was offering. Even worse, some of the clients for whom he did work later failed to pay.

Rick was discouraged. He decided to try to go back to a full-time job. But while he was pursuing his false starts, the carnage in his industry had continued. He was competing with many other people much like himself for jobs that could easily disappear the next week.

This is where Rick was when I first met him at an organization of local business consultants. When he told me of his belief that banks had downsized much of their expertise, I suggested that he might be able to sell his services as a contractor, who could take on specific projects or manage certain operations for banks on a contract basis. He still had plenty of good contacts in the industry. He thought it was worth a try.

He had a measure of success in this consultant/contractor role, but it quickly started to wear him down. He spent a lot of time trying to sell banks a highly specific service they often didn't need.

One day, after Rick had made yet another unsuccessful pitch, the prospective client began thinking out loud. A key person in the bank, a woman with highly specialized skills, was about to go on maternity leave. He told Rick that her absence would cause a real problem, and he wondered if there was anyone who might work temporarily, as Rick had offered to do, while she was away.

By this time, Rick knew hundreds of downsized banking professionals. After a few minutes of thought, he was able to come up with several seasoned candidates who could take over this specialized task almost immediately.

He was able to solve this banker's problem without much effort, and that got him thinking. He realized that he knew experienced professionals who could plug into virtually any important slot in the banking industry. Rather than sell just his own specialty, he could sell the services of bankers in all specialties.

Rick's insight seems, in retrospect, to have been a fairly obvious one. Temporary professional staffing and outsourcing have, after all, been among the most notable business trends of the 1990s. Yet in 1995, when Rick began his business, nobody else in his business and regional market had figured it out—nobody, that is, who had Rick's knowledge, experience and contacts.

While Rick's earlier efforts had sputtered, Schilling Professional Staffing Inc. took off more quickly than he had ever imagined. The last time I talked to him, Rick had 2500 banking professionals in his database, and was regularly placing them in highly responsible, well-paying, temporary jobs.

The banker who worried about losing his key staffer didn't intend to give Rick a valuable idea. He was merely telling Rick what the bank really needed. Fortunately, Rick was listening.

Getting over getting fired

One of the most common mistakes is to ignore good news. That's particularly easy to do when it comes on the heels of a disaster. Nevertheless, fixating on failure can make you oblivious to the seeds of your future success.

One Monday morning at nine o'clock, John Carey was fired. There had been no warning. He had, of course, seen many of his colleagues laid off in the months before, shed so that his company would gain a leaner, more dynamic image. But he thought that he was specialized and safe, at least for a few years more.

Many people in John's position would immediately begin to look for another job. He was convinced, however, that another job wasn't for him. It wasn't yet ten o'clock when he began to write a business plan. He had had some experience, years before, of working for and running small businesses. He resolved that he was never going to be an employee again.

However, beginning to write the plan is not the same as getting anything done. John sat there trying to write, making a number of false starts, never seeming to get anywhere. He knew more or less what he wanted to do: to make use of the specialized employee-training techniques he had developed for his employer and sell them to others. But the thoughts did not cohere, the words did not come, he could not arrive at a vision for how his business would work.

On his second day of grappling futilely with the business plan, he received an email. It was from a friend who had heard what had happened to John. He had some work he wanted John to do. It was something that John could do well, just the sort of thing he might have included in his business plan, had he been able to write it.

Even then, the knowledge that he would have income and something to do—that his business was already off to a good start, in other words—did not help

John to imagine what this business would be. He sat at the computer but could not write a word. What should he say he was doing? What should he call his business? He had some answers, but none of them seemed right. His spirits sank lower and lower and lower.

Finally, he was able to talk himself out of this impasse by simply walking away from the task. Starting to write a business plan an hour after being fired, he decided, was not a way of addressing his problem, but rather a way of denying it. His job had been a very good one, with a good salary and good benefits. He had believed he was very good at what he did.

He had put years of his life into working for that company, and suddenly all the imagination and passion he had invested in his work had been judged valueless. Part of his life had perished that Monday morning, and he had denied himself the time to mourn. He decided that he needed to put his emotions first and deal with the loss before he tried to define what would happen next in his life.

John needed time to realize that one big change in his life was that he would not have the apparent security and predictability of life as an employee. At the least, he became properly grateful that work had materialized right away, and opted, for the moment, to allow that experience to guide him. "I decided," he said, "to let the marketplace tell me what is needed rather than try to force myself to come up with a detailed idea right away."

He realized that he had been avoiding socializing, even though talking with others is one of the best ways to develop or clarify ideas. As he opened himself up to uncertainty, he was able to stop hiding. He felt his anger subside. He was able to think soberly.

That's when he realized that there were things that were more important to his business than a detailed business plan. He bought health insurance, purchased a computer, looked for an office, then settled in his spare bedroom when that option proved too costly.

When I talked with him, he still didn't have a business plan but he did have work. Indeed, one of his clients is the company that fired him. It still values his expertise, only on a part-time basis. He's happy to have the work, but he doesn't see it as vindication. He has come to terms with that loss in his life, and is finally ready to move on.

Pennies from heaven

When I set up my business in 1983, I had expectations that proved to be completely upside down. I believed it would be a long time before I would be able to build up a regular demand for my services. Thus, to tide me over, I developed a surefire product that would generate substantial income from Day One.

This was a list of Chinese libraries that buy foreign books and journals. I knew from experience that such a list would be very useful to publishing companies, and that my list was better than any other.

As I was completing the list, I wrote a promotion letter and mailed it to hundreds of publishers. I had rented a post office box to receive the anticipated deluge of prepaid orders. I was perturbed that only the smallest post office box was available; overflow might well be a problem.

A few weeks went by. I managed to acquire three clients for my services, almost immediately, and I became quite busy. Still, I found time to go to the post office twice daily to pick up the checks for the list. The problem was that there weren't any. All I ever found was junk mail.

Then one day, I received an envelope from something called the Center for UFO Studies, an organization to which I hadn't written. I almost threw it away unopened, but then I notice that it contained a check. It was for $50, a rental fee for only a tiny portion of the mailing list. I deposited the check in the bank. It cleared!

It wasn't much money, but it was the first income the list ever generated. And it had come, literally, from out of the blue, from people who were searching for something that might not, in fact, exist. While it was nice to make some money, I was nevertheless troubled by it. Was my business based on a delusion, a need that nobody else could see? Were believers in extraterrestrial visitors the only people who would believe in me?

Eventually, I did find companies that paid for my list. I have continued to update and greatly expand it, and several of the largest publishers in the world lease it regularly. But the number of checks I receive has still never strained the capacity of my mailbox.

As it has turned out, the most important thing about the list is that it has made people aware of me. It transpired that my skills are more valuable to many companies than my list, and a few list buyers have become important clients for my services. Some have also taken me in new directions. One, the American Management Association, hired me to create a course for executives on doing business in China, which has led in turn to further opportunities to brief executives and launch training programs for multinational companies. Although the list has never made me rich—or even contributed a significant percentage of my annual income—it has opened doors to opportunities I couldn't have dreamed of.

I thought when I created the list that I had invented a better mousetrap, and that the world would beat a path to my door. What I had really done was to plant a tree, which, after years of cultivation, has borne abundant fruit.

The list is a good product, but it couldn't have worked for me as it has if I had not persevered and kept upgrading and promoting it, and myself, along the way. Money doesn't fall from the sky. And on those rare occasions when it does, it's not enough to live on.

Struggle.com

Ideas have a very short shelf life today. Most of us have been brought up to believe that persistence will be rewarded, and often it is. But it can be a big mistake to be too wedded to one clearly defined idea when circumstances are telling you to try something else.

Jeff Tannenbaum and Brett Cohen are in the midst of starting their third business in three years. The first, which they started as college roommates, was a service to wake up people like themselves, who had been working at their computers all night, in time to get to class. They were literally entangled in their venture. Cables sprouted across their sofa, around their desks and in front of the television. The thing was, though, that it worked. There were enough other reluctant risers on campus to give them a satisfactory cashflow. They were in business!

Then they decided to look for a way to create a larger business that would appeal to their cyberspace-seasoned peers around the nation and the world. Their idea was a ride-sharing bulletin board that would not only help college students find free or inexpensive transportation, but would also put people in touch with one another. One morning in the shower, Brett came up with what he thought was the perfect name: collegefriends.com. Thus they had a concept. They were confident of their technology. They thought their name was a winner.

Given what has happened since on the internet, you might assume that this is the story of a couple of boy billionaires. It's not, at least not yet. What they didn't have was the capital required to make the idea a reality. Nor did they have the good fortune to encounter any investors who subscribed to the theory that, on the business frontier of the internet, being first is far more important than knowing exactly when and how you are going to make a profit.

Brett and Jeff were both 21 years old and still undergraduates. To those considering funding them, they looked like kids, and not necessarily geniuses. Jeff recalls, "They would say, 'Who are you? You're half my age, and you're trying to get me to invest in you?'" Jeff and Brett's biggest obstacles were men with graying hair—people like me, in other words. The two partners were certain that these people didn't really have a clue about how things work in a wired world.

The pair's make-or-break-it moment came when they obtained an introduction to an investor whom they were told could provide the $500,000 to $750,000 that would be required to get collegefriends.com on the road. Day and night they prepared for the meeting. They honed their presentation. They made slides. They repeated the demo over and over again to make sure it worked. They took their suits to the cleaners. They ironed their shirts. They practiced being serious and businesslike. They impressed each other enormously.

When the day of the presentation came, the gray-haired investor looked attentive and interested, until, about midway through, he whispered something to a colleague who had come with him, and they both laughed loudly.

Jeff and Brett were devastated. They hadn't made a joke, or even said anything remotely clever. They didn't dare because they were trying to be so serious. But it was difficult to complete the presentation once their prospect had laughed. "At the end, he said what a good product he thought it was," Jeff recalls. But he didn't offer to invest any money. Instead, he said, the two should go to the Wharton School's small business development center for help in preparing a better business plan.

Jeff and Brett believed that the expert polishing Wharton might offer would add nothing to the merits of the business, and it would take time they knew they didn't have. On the internet, concepts wilt faster than arugula. In 1997, they aborted the project and, after they graduated from college, both took well-paying jobs.

Within a year, two other companies went on the internet with concepts similar to collegefriends.com, though neither is the new amazon.com. After a few months, Jeff, who was working for a telecommunications company, decided that he needed to be in business again, and he convinced Brett to join him. The two founded

DreamFront, a concept involving interactive, internet-based entertainment, though they were reluctant to be specific. It is a more ambitious business than their previous one, and they are working night and day on it. The climate for capitalizing internet concepts has improved, and Jeff and Brett are out looking for some venturesome money.

They are older, but not much older, starting again, confident that they have a world-beating idea. And if that doesn't work, it seems inevitable that they will have another and another.

Both Jeff and Brett know that plenty of employers will pay highly for their skills, though they are determined to find a way to remain independent. Nevertheless, the condescension of the gray-haired capitalist who laughed still rankles. "I intend," Jeff says, "to be the person laughing all the way to the bank."

A CEO no more

One of the most shocking things about leaving a corporate job and setting out in business on your own is the realization of how alone you are. In the corporation you play a role. Its hierarchy provides an identity. Your job often gives you a profile in your community. You may not like the corporation or respect your fellow workers, but whether you know it or not, being employed offers reassurances that go far beyond a paycheck.

Once you are on your own, the world seems to pay no attention to you at all. And when it does, it is only to ask, "Who the hell are you?"

Dick Signorelli was the chief executive officer of a chemical company, with sales of about $200 million a year and plants in the US and UK. He was a hands-on executive, someone who took pride in his visibility on the factory floor, dealing with workers at every level of the company. Nevertheless, he was the boss, and he had become accustomed to having a responsive staff of talented people dedicated to carrying out his desires.

He admits that even as he looked forward to a time when he would not bear such heavy responsibilities, he had never quite considered what life would be like once he stopped being the boss. He foresaw a new, more leisurely, more flexible career in which he would spend his time sharing his expertise in strategic management and corporate turnarounds with other executives and students.

What he never expected was that the deference to which he had been accustomed would end, and that he would suffer treatment that bordered on contempt. Moreover, he had never imagined how powerless he would feel to deal with such behavior.

The incident that brought this painful feeling home to Dick happened at an event that appeared, at first, to be the entrée to exactly the sort of career he had imagined. It was a five-day workshop for top executives from several different companies. He had been asked to prepare himself to be the leader for one of the days, with the understanding that if he did well, he would lead entire sessions on his own.

He worked hard to prepare his presentation, which he outlined extensively on his computer using the PowerPoint presentation program. However, he was concerned that he might repeat what the principal leader had already said. So he asked both the person who had asked him to come and the principal leader if they would like to look through his presentation, but both declined.

The night before Dick was to make his presentation, the leader changed his mind. He came to Dick's hotel room at 10 o'clock to look at the presentation on his laptop computer. He told Dick that it was good, though he had some changes to recommend. Dick let the man sit down at the keyboard and do some work.

A few minutes later, the leader told Dick that there was a problem. He had inadvertently, he said, destroyed the entire presentation on Dick's computer. He offered a perfunctory apology, then told Dick not to worry. Rather than do an entire day of presentation, Dick could stand up for 15 minutes. The leader would be able to handle the rest.

Dick was flabbergasted. He was infuriated. Unfortunately, he was also speechless. He believed himself to be the victim of a blatant and willful act of sabotage, but he didn't want to sully himself by confronting this man who had revealed himself to be Dick's adversary.

When the man left his room, Dick called a friend who told him how to recover the computer file. Technically, he hadn't been defeated. He had his full day of presentation notes.

But the next morning, he could not rouse himself to confront the leader. He sat at the back of the room for the entire day, until, late in the afternoon, the leader invited him to stand up and speak for 15 minutes. And that was that.

Dick packed up his computer and went home, having learned that, when he's in business for himself, even an ex-CEO is just another guy.

❖❖❖

The world is full of information for the new spare room tycoon, though it's not always easy to understand what reality is telling you. Customers, clients, and income are good indications that you are heading in the right direction. But valuable information can also come hidden as bad news. When things don't work, don't panic. Figure out why. And when good results come from areas where you weren't expecting them, listen to what the market is telling you.

No matter how carefully you have tried to plan, things won't work out as you expect. Your business has been born, but it is not yet what it will become. You can barely imagine what that might be. That's what makes it thrilling.

Succeeding

4
Making the Sale

First, make the sale. Identify and woo the customers. Let the world know what you have to offer.

Every would-be independent business person knows this advice. And although not all of us feel comfortable promoting ourselves, we know—in our minds if not in our guts—that we have to do it.

Something that fewer people know is that we have to keep doing it, even when our business is successful.

It's an effort for all of us. We might observe that someone is "a born salesperson." But while it's true that some personalities adapt to selling better than others, selling is a skill you must develop, a habit you must cultivate.

That doesn't mean that you need to become a fast-talking con artist, or that you should overpromise to close the deal. You didn't go independent in order to become someone you don't respect; besides, it's bad business in the long run. But you have to get used to communicating the benefits of what you offer, and to looking for opportunities everywhere.

When spare room tycoons talk to each other, a common subject is the breakthrough—the big thing that takes the business to another level. For a software startup, it might be the decision of a multinational company to license your product. For a lawyer, a recruiter or a marketing researcher, it might be a long-term retainer with a high-profile client. For someone introducing a new food product, it is a place on the shelves of a giant supermarket chain.

Like fishermen, we have a tendency to talk about the big one that got away. We speak of the breakthrough that almost happened, or the one that's just beyond the horizon. Implicit in this dream of the really big breakthrough is the belief that, once it happens, we won't have to worry about the survival of our business ever again.

There is a danger in all this talk about big breakthroughs: It may lead us to undervalue the little breakthroughs, the day-to-day business that pays the bills, puts food on the table, and keeps us going. My experience is that small customers are usually more reliable sources of income, and their money is just as good.

Breakthroughs do happen, of course. They happen to everyone who keeps selling, responding to the marketplace and imagining new ways for people to profit from what you offer. You need breakthroughs, and you are fully entitled to celebrate when they happen.

Don't jump to the conclusion that you are a genius, however. You may be benefiting from one of the strong tides of fashion that move through every field and quickly fade away. You may have blundered into the right place at the right time. If you can't figure out how you got there, you'll find yourself in the wrong place at the wrong time soon enough.

You will learn that one breakthrough isn't enough. Nor are two or four or eight. Through no fault of your own, you will lose important customers. Companies merge, executives switch jobs, tastes change. The only way you can deal with these desertions is to make sure that you have new business coming in. No matter how many breakthroughs you have, you need to keep marketing yourself.

This is difficult when business is strong, because you feel that you cannot take the time. It may be even more difficult, though, when business is weak, because you are aware that expanding your customer base might be a matter of life or death. Nobody will have confidence in you if you seem desperate.

Promoting your business isn't just for bad times. And it's not just for good times. It is for all times.

Selling is like breathing

When I was a child in Hong Kong, my father was a wholesaler and importer of luggage and my mother ran a store whose offerings ranged from women's underwear to toys to toilet paper to Pond's Cold Cream. I grew up in the store selling anything to anyone who wandered in. This retail upbringing, in hindsight, trained me as a salesman without my knowing it.

As a teenager, I wanted to be a scholar. No member of my family had ever gone to college. I was able to win admission to the University of Hong Kong, which accepted only a tiny fraction of those who sought entrance. Later, I got into the University of Chicago, got my master's degree and then went to the University of

Michigan in Ann Arbor and obtained my PhD. All these degrees were very important in terms of training me how to write, read, think, imagine, articulate, and compete.

But it was my parents' store that best prepared me for the life I now lead. To succeed on your own, you must learn how to sell. You must convince people that you are the answer to their problems, that you have the knowledge and skill that will help them reach their goal.

It's easier to sell a product than it is to sell your own services. Telling people how good you are feels immodest, even aggressive. And it's easy to communicate any discomfort to those you're trying to convince. Yet you have no choice but to learn to sell. For those who've made their vows to stop being corporate courtiers and become wandering warriors of capitalism, selling should be a reflex.

In the beginning, we might sell just a little too aggressively. Our eyes are open a bit too wide, our voices are strident, our faces stiff. We are too self-conscious about selling ourselves.

It's important to remember that you're not truly selling yourself, but rather the help you can offer, the solutions you can provide. In a way, it's just as if you're selling face creams or mousetraps. What you have to offer is something you know will do the job. The product you're selling is not who you truly are, but rather the job you can do. Separating yourself from the service or product you offer makes it easier to accept rejection. If people don't buy, it's not because you're a bad person. Rather, it's because they don't think they need what you are offering. If you were a better salesperson, you might have convinced them otherwise. But just because you didn't doesn't mean you're a less worthy person. Once you understand that, you can relax while you're selling, which will probably make you more effective.

This is easy to say, difficult to achieve. Don't lose heart. It all comes with practice. I now know that when I began, people probably thought I was a nuisance and a charlatan. But I have had the opportunity over the years to prove to many clients—and to myself—that I can accomplish what I promise. My mere survival has prompted people to look at me differently. People who once showed disdain toward me began to show respect. They even started to like me. To my great surprise, they have come to consider me a guru.

In essence, if you fight a hundred battles, you may not be the boldest or bravest warrior; but at least you have shown that you are skilled enough to survive. And if you endure over time, and maintain your self-respect, you will win the respect of others. You will prevail.

Fear of selling

One of the chief things spare room tycoons are looking for is integrity. If we do things we don't approve of, we can't claim that anyone else made us act in that manner. Selling doesn't have to be sleazy. It's a way to let people know about something they can use. Yet many independents fixate on the bad experiences we have had with salespeople and resist doing what they need to do to survive.

Bill Frysinger knows that he has no choice but to learn how to sell. If he doesn't let people know about the value of his services as an electronics product development engineer and designer of theater sound systems, nobody else will.

Bill ran his own company for several years, then took a series of full-time jobs, and is now back on his own again. Though he realizes that he has to communicate with potential clients in order to find out what they need, and let them know he can do it, he finds himself confronting a deep prejudice against selling.

Indeed, one of the reasons he wants to be on his own is that he believed that, too often, his former employers' sales and marketing staffs, and even their top executives, regularly tried to win business by promising more than they could reasonably expect to deliver. It was, in a sense, a vote of confidence in engineers like Bill that these execs had faith that they would be able to come up with something to solve the client's problem. But in Bill's eyes, it was really an act of bad faith.

"I'd rather that they fire me than for me to sign my name on a piece of paper that states that we can deliver what we cannot," he says. Moreover, such behavior makes it difficult, Bill feels, for someone who deals honestly to compete.

"We product development engineers are used to 'underselling,' promising even less than we know we can deliver," Bill observes. "That's because the marketing people are used to trumpeting performance of, say, 120 percent of what they know they can deliver. We engineers downplay our capabilities so that what gets promised is more or less what we are able to do." Thus, even when he is being absolutely on the level, Bill tends to feel that he is boasting.

Bill has decided to deal with his sales phobia in an interesting way. He has volunteered to be a fundraiser for a charity. "When I do fundraising, I know I'm selling," he says. "But I don't feel like a stereotypical salesman because I'm selling something I believe in, not myself."

The next step, in Bill's view, is to be able to see what he offers not as an overblown image of himself but as something his clients need. "I'm not willing to fit the image I have of most salespeople," he says. So he is trying to find a way to prove to himself that he can sell honestly and enthusiastically—and still feel good about it the next morning.

Small customers, big ideas

I am told that there is a Yiddish saying—not so much a proverb as a cry of faithful exasperation—that translates as "God will provide. If only He would provide until He provides."

That's a feeling most spare room tycoons have occasionally. We believe that things will come out all right. After all, we had the courage to start our own businesses. We are confident the breakthrough will come, if only we can live so long.

This thinking tends to undervalue the smaller customers, the ones who actually do provide our livelihoods until the breakthrough comes. Marketing guru Stan Gross spent years trying to get Madison Avenue and multinationals to pay attention. But he survived, and learned a lot, by working for small family-owned companies. When the multinationals were finally ready, Stan was prepared as well.

Stan believes that he was destined to be in business on his own. "I have always had the desire to call my own shots," he says. "I have always had the drive to greater rewards. I have always had to have more thrills than most people." Those three characteristics, says psychologist Gross, are part of the mental makeup of people who run their own businesses, or at least of those who keep at it.

But destiny is one thing, and survival is another. Stan, whose firm has helped Coca-Cola, McDonald's, DuPont and many other companies explore the "inner minds" of consumers, had to keep at it for a long time. By his account, the lean years stretched from 1970 to 1986.

He began his career at a high level, rising quickly to a marketing executive position at a New York company, while at the same time consulting with large firms, and doing high profile *pro bono* work promoting President John F. Kennedy's physical fitness campaign. Among his mentors was the cosmetics magnate Charles Revson— one of the founders of Revlon—who advised him to get out of management and into a business of his own.

After he went back to school for advanced degrees in psychology and marketing, and a few years spent teaching, Stan finally did set up his own business. Friends and family advised him to keep teaching and to consult on the side, but he felt that it wouldn't be fair to his students to do so because his business needed all his energy. Yet he quickly found that the doors that had been open to him as a young man were closed to him now that he really had something good to offer.

"When I would get interviews with people from big companies, it seemed as if they would just sit there, as if I hadn't spoken at all, as if I had lost my ability to communicate," he recalls. "Here I was trying to advise people on communication, and I wasn't getting through at all. More than once I finished one of these presentations, and just went back to my car and cried."

One day he went to New York, to the offices of Bristol-Meyers Squibb, and called executives whose names he had researched from the telephone booth in the lobby. He had papers spread all over the floor around the telephone, and at one point he thought he was going to be evicted from the building, not invited upstairs. But eventually, the director of market research agreed to see him.

When Stan had finished his pitch, the executive told him that his work was interesting, sensational even. But he said Stan would get no work from Bristol-Meyers Squibb because his work didn't fit into the way the company did things and as director of research, the executive wasn't about to go out on a limb to change things.

The clients who sustained Stan's business during the lean years weren't in New York but in Lancaster, Pennsylvania. They were owners of small companies who were impressed by Stan's background, and didn't seem to understand how unusual his approach was. Marketing research was a new thing for these business people, most of whom had grown up in Amish families, about as far from the reach of Madison Avenue advertising culture as one can get in the US. Work for these small companies was his internship, Stan says. They kept food on the family table, and helped him learn how to work so that he could perform when opportunities came.

Prepared to succeed

Opportunities are often what we define them to be. Spare room tycoons are frequently faced not with well-defined challenges, but with ambiguous situations. What we make of such chances can change everything.

On one level, Mike McGrail's story, which begins with an encounter at church, sounds like someone who was touched by an angel. Mike doesn't see it that way. Rather, he believes that the key to his success was reacting boldly and imaginatively to an opportunity that many people might not have recognized. He grabbed the chance and thought big.

Mike spent the first two decades of his adult life working for some of the largest companies on earth. When the multinational for which he was working re-engineered him out of a job, he quickly hooked up with an exciting startup that grew quickly into a 6000-employee company. When that company was acquired, many of those employees were out of a job and Mike was among them.

Even when he had been working as a top manager in these large companies, Mike had encouraged his wife Mary to start independent businesses—as a stockbroker, a real estate professional, and finally a trainer. After his second downsizing, Mike and Mary purchased a franchise to train executives how to be better leaders. They also offered training in job fit assessment, psychological testing, and time management, among other areas. The first few years were difficult. Even though he was able to bring in gross fees of more than $100,000, his overhead and marketing costs were large.

In fact, much of the McGrail Group's business came from selling services to friends and neighbors, many of whom were executives. (It can pay to live in an upscale neighborhood.) These referrals were generating other word-of-mouth recommendations. In short, the trends were positive, but in order to prosper, Mike and Mary needed a breakthrough.

Mike is a religious man, active in his church. He decided to become a lector, one who reads scripture to the congregation, so he signed up for a training course that the church was offering. During a break in the session, all the participants went to the church basement for refreshments. Mike sat down at a table by himself, not thinking much of anything. Then another lector trainee sat down beside him and asked Mike what he did for a living. "I own a management training company," Mike replied, and the man's eyes lit up.

"Here's my card," he said. "Give me a call Monday morning." Mike looked at the card. The stranger was general manager of a large company known for caring about its employees, just the kind of company Mike and Mary needed for a breakthrough.

The first time they met, the general manager told Mike that he had a vision for radically changing the company's operations and the way it assessed its results, but that he had been frustrated because people within the company were unresponsive. The second time they met, he gave Mike a job, but it was a disappointing one. It involved one-on-one training with only one vice-president. This was far from the breakthrough his business required, but he did the work to everyone's satisfaction, and hoped for more. It didn't come.

The general manager was quite cordial when Mike came to make his pitch for more work. Later, though, he interrupted Mike in mid-sentence by throwing a book on the table. "Did you read this?" he asked. The book was *The Goal* by Eli Goldratt, an examination of synchronized manufacturing.

Mike was embarrassed to have to say he hadn't, especially since the book's subject was one in which he claimed expertise. But he told the client that he would read it and get back to him. When he read the book, he realized that he had been issued an important, though unspoken, invitation. The client wanted to make major changes at the company, this book suggested their direction, and in the course of his discussions with the client, he had gleaned a great deal of information about how the company worked.

Mike returned to the client not with a mere reaction, but with a detailed proposal for putting Goldratt's ideas to work in order to solve the specific operational problems the general manager had been discussing. Although Mike wasn't trained as a manufacturing engineer, he realized that just about every step in his career had prepared him to work on this task. Mike's proposal outlined how to make the most of his own expertise, as well as that of others he planned to draw on. The client accepted his proposal, a six-month project that involved an immense amount of work. As a result, the client was able to achieve a 50 percent inventory reduction, which had an immediate positive impact on the bottom line.

Mike's experience made him an expert in an area he was well qualified for, but had never thought of entering. And when Mike's client was absorbed by a larger company, for once it was good news for Mike. His program has been put to work in the UK, France, Brazil, China, Spain and elsewhere, generating new billing and new opportunities for him. He began training one employee, and now has changed the lives of thousands and helped make the company's products competitive in construction markets worldwide.

For Mike, the moral of this story is: "You have to be prepared to be successful." But he also sees it as a story about flexibility, the willingness to explore different kinds of business opportunities you haven't foreseen. A business plan is useful, but if it's too restrictive, it can blind you to opportunities that you're well equipped to realize.

Mike didn't go to church to find a client; he went because he always did. And if there is something faintly miraculous in this story, it is that his eventual client seemed from the beginning to see something in Mike that Mike hadn't yet discovered in himself.

Waking to opportunity

When you're trying to generate business, there are plenty of times when nothing seems to work. You have a prospective client who seems really to need what you do. You prepare yourself for the meeting, and you feel that you're incisive, and eloquent, and worth every penny you're asking. You even feel that you have established a rapport with the prospective client. Yet, even though you've done everything right, nothing happens.

On those occasions when it feels like you can't win, it's worth remembering those times when everything went right—despite what you did.

I hope that I'll never mess up worse than I did one morning when I had been in business for less than a year. One of the companies that responded to a mailing was a company located in Connecticut, about three hours by train from my base in Philadelphia. I didn't entirely understand what they did, but I heard the enthusiasm in the caller's voice, and I arranged a mid-morning appointment the following week. As long as I could make the 6:40 am train from Thirtieth Street Station, everything would be fine.

The day before I was to go, I received a very welcome call. A good friend with whom I had worked in New York was in the Philadelphia area, interviewing for a job. She had been out of work for a while, so this was really great news. I invited her to come to dinner and to stay the night. By the time she arrived, the news was even better. She had been offered the job. That called for a celebration. We opened a bottle of something, then a bottle of something else. We chattered on about old times, gossiped about our old co-workers, speculated about where she might live. We went on for hours and hours and then even more hours. By the time I finally went to bed, it was clear I was going to get only about four hours' sleep, at best.

Fortunately I was able to catnap on the train, but when I arrived in Greenwich I was still in a fog. The president of the company greeted me personally, and took me back to headquarters, where he seated me in front of a computer monitor and demonstrated his product. I stared at the monitor uncomprehendingly as he droned on.

Then I did something that terrified me: I woke up. As I was suddenly startled into consciousness, and figured out where I was, I realized that I had actually drifted off to sleep as the company president was talking to me. Things like this happen to me in nightmares, but usually I can escape them by waking up. Not this time. To this day, I don't know how long I had dozed. I assume I didn't snore.

Yet, as I shocked myself into alertness, I realized that the president seemed not to have noticed, or at least chose to ignore, that I had been sleeping through his pronouncements. Indeed, he seemed more to be selling me on doing work for his company than evaluating whether I was the right person to do the job. I stayed awake long enough to let him know I'd be happy to do the project he had in mind. This led in turn to a year's retainer, and a trip to China with the president. I never asked him whether he had noticed that I had missed most of our first meeting.

This is not a success story I ever hope to repeat, and I've made sure that I have never done so. I am still embarrassed at my behavior that morning. Still, it offers a lesson that took me many years to learn: When people want you, they'll find a reason to value you. But when you're trying to sell your services to people who are not ready to use it, you'll never win regardless of how logical, useful, valuable, or perfect you are. I had proved to myself that the cliché is true: Nothing beats being at the right place at the right time—even if you're asleep when you get there.

Your first client is yourself

Not until quite recently, perhaps only a year or two ago, did I actually sit down and write a marketing plan for myself. I'd been planning to do it for years, more than a decade actually. But something—anything—else always seemed to be more urgent.

Independents are reluctant to work for themselves: doing the kind of planning, marketing, training, financial analysis and other internal tasks that are essential to the survival of any business. That's because we get paid to work for others. We don't get paid to work for ourselves.

Besides, many people go on their own in order to indulge their creativity—as a chef, a writer, an artisan or even an international trade consultant. Have you ever wondered, while scanning the obituaries, whether you will be remembered for something you have done? I remember reading once about the first man who ever sold popcorn in cinemas. He was a truly obscure man, but he had affected the lives of millions, and he changed the economics of the movie theater business along the way. Most of us would like to be remembered not as a bank balance, but as someone who made a difference in the world.

Writing a marketing or a financial plan is not such an act. These are routine tasks that generate more routines: researching potential clients, creating mailing lists, addressing envelopes, poring over spreadsheets. They can be tedious activities, especially when you know that nobody's paying you to do them. Many of us will put off such tasks until business slows down. By then, the trend lines are already going in the wrong direction. Tasks which are, under better circumstances, merely dreary now become fraught with anxiety. You start to tell yourself that this promotional mailing has to work, because you can't afford it if it fails.

After all these years of being on my own, I have finally lived through enough ups and downs to realize that I have to work for my own business, indeed that I am my most demanding and time-consuming client. The future of my business depends on my continuing to market my services even when times are good. My marketing plan is not a philosophical document; it's more like a "to do" list. It establishes a routine. Even now, I still must force myself to follow it and stick to the plan, even when there seems to be no time or energy left.

I'm reluctant to hire others to do these tasks because they don't have an immediate payoff. Maybe in a few more years, I'll decide that I can afford to. Even if I do, there are still some parts of this job—showing up at public events, keeping in touch with former clients and other business associates, deciding how to market your products or services—that only the proprietor can do. I've found that one of the most powerful actions I can take is to be out and about, reminding people I'm still in business.

Finding new customers means we have to kiss thousands of frogs—and just as many next month. We can never be sure which ones will turn out to be a princess or a prince. Two things are certain: Doing all that kissing is a royal pain in the behind. And no spare room tycoon can afford to stop doing it.

❖❖❖

When you're in business for yourself, scarcely a day goes by without you selling. If you don't sell, you don't survive. Some find this dispiriting. I'm among those who find it energizing to get other people excited about what I do. Even so, I have had to design a regimen to make sure I do this marketing.

Even when we are making money hand over fist, we must discipline ourselves to devote time to promote our business. It is easier to promote when you don't feel that your survival depends on immediate success.

Many spare room tycoons complain that when they are busy, they have no time to market their products and services. As a result, when the flurry of activity ends, there is no business to take its place. Few spare room tycoons are able to escape this feast or famine pattern entirely, but it is important to try.

Promoting your business is a long-term investment. Some customers may take one or two years to come through. And it is important to remind potential customers of your continued presence, so that they will think of you when they need what you offer.

Many people don't like to promote themselves, and being busy seems to provide an excuse to duck this chore. Many more businesses fail because they have too few customers than because there are too many. To any sane spare room tycoon, there is no such thing as having too many customers.

You can never afford to stop selling.

5
Confidence Is Money

There is no greater asset for a spare room tycoon than an absolute conviction that you know what you're doing. If you don't feel sure of yourself, why should anyone else trust you?

This is obvious. But for most of us, confidence is something that comes and goes. What's more, it often vanishes unexpectedly, just when you need it most. When I feel confident, everything seems to work better. When I feel insecure, nothing goes right. I become self-conscious. I begin to doubt my own abilities, and mistrust other people as well.

While confidence is useful for everyone, it is particularly vital when you are in business for yourself. When you work for a company, your very position gives you a sense of legitimacy. Spare room tycoons stand on our own, and we mustn't be seen to be quivering in our high heels or wing tips. We demand to be taken seriously. Everything about us should inspire trust.

In his influential book *Learned Optimism*, psychologist Martin Seligman cites scientific data showing that pessimistic people have a firmer grasp on reality than people with a sunnier outlook. The optimists, however, are likely to be happier, healthier, and more successful. Seligman argues that, for most people, it's worth learning to be optimistic. It's good for you.

Obviously, you can't stay in business if you don't have a grasp on reality, and especially on how things are changing. Yet, it is the nature of the spare room tycoon not to accept reality without a bit of a fight. We are, after all, in business to change the world, not simply to accept things as they are. Our success depends on a good helping of presumptuousness. We are remaking the world to our liking. But we will never succeed unless we are convinced—and unless we appear convinced—that what we are doing will succeed.

Everyone has moments of insecurity. Indeed, many of the stories in this book relate the impact of self-doubt on the lives of independent business people. Confidence is a quality that comes and goes, but, as several of the stories that follow suggest, it is also a discipline that can be learned. And if you can succeed in learning confidence, you will not simply be happier and healthier, but wealthier besides.

Building self-assurance

By now, you have read enough of these lessons to know that spare room tycoons tend to love their autonomy, but are often dogged by insecurity.

Even so, I wasn't expecting when I went to visit Ellen Thompson, founder and CEO of a company called Know It All Inc., that we'd be talking about how difficult, and important, it is to maintain your confidence.

Ellen has plenty to be confident about. Her product—a software system that allows people to take tests of their computer and office skills anywhere in the world, over the internet, and be graded instantly—is a winner. She has more than 2000 customers, including some of the world's largest and best-known companies.

She was only 22 when she started the company with a mere $7000 in savings. Six years later, she has turned down millions of dollars to sell it. She is the person countless startup entrepreneurs would like to become, and fast.

Ellen didn't set up her company to sell this product. Rather, while trying to develop a business to tutor users of popular software programs, she realized how useful such a product would be. She hired people to develop the program and make it work. Her education, which combined business and engineering, gave her an edge, she believes, in turning her good idea into a reality.

However, what she wanted to talk about, it turned out, was not her success, but rather the discipline required to maintain her confidence. Confidence is an asset that doesn't appear on the balance sheet, although Ellen is convinced that it is reflected in the bottom line.

Recently, she says, she sat in on another entrepreneur's presentation to a venture capital firm. The numbers on the charts he presented were much less impressive than those Ellen could present. But she found herself being drawn in, like the venture capitalists themselves, by the self-assurance with which the man made the presentation. The way he stood, the expression on his face, the sound of his voice all contributed to making his business plan seem less risky and more valuable.

"I think that women are more prone to feeling insecure than men," she says. "Society gives us clues which make us feel that we are second-class citizens. Men look perfectly fine with gray hair, but a woman with gray hair is considered a washout. I don't look like a Barbie doll. I don't look like I've jumped out of a page from *Vogue* or *Mademoiselle*."

Ellen admits that this is a familiar complaint, but she believes that for a female business owner, the anxieties produced by this double standard can have serious economic consequences.

"When you have self-doubts, you can be walking into a loss," she says. "If you know your business is worth $10 million, but if you're worrying that you won't get that figure and ask for $5 million, then $5 million is what you'll get."

Ellen's ability to throw millions around like this, even in conversation, betrays a degree of confidence many spare room tycoons never achieve. She says that's because she works on her confidence continually.

"Successful entrepreneurs have to have a well-developed sense of self," she says. And, she argues, it is not nearly enough to be intelligent. "It's like martial arts," she says. "There's no guarantee that because you're athletic, you'll make a good marital arts fighter. You have to practice every day to get good at it."

Business as a contact sport

We often think of confidence as an intangible, largely psychic phenomenon. Yet as Mario Sikora demonstrates, confidence often rests on a physical basis.

Mario works as an executive coach and corporate team-building trainer. Powerful, well-paid executives come to him so he can help them to project their power and to move and act with authority. Mario, who used to be a karate instructor, says the top executives come to him for the same reason his martial arts students did—in order to gain an edge.

When Mario was a boy, he felt small and timid. He was tormented by a bully who lived across the street. The problem became so bad that he urged his parents to let him take karate lessons. After a few months, he dropped the lessons, but he decided to fight back against the bully. Mario was beaten badly, but even so, the bully didn't take the risk of ridiculing or threatening him as he had before.

Another incident the following year really changed Mario's attitude. He was playing ice hockey, and another bully took the opportunity to attack him as if it were part of the game. Mario found himself flying head over heels across the rink, somersaulting in mid-air and landing face down. As he climbed to his knees, with his face bleeding, he made a decision. "I said to myself, 'Nobody is ever going to hit me again,'" he recalls. "I was determined to be comfortable in front of people in every way."

Mario went back to his martial arts training and earned a black belt in kempo karate. He was also fortunate that his hormones finally kicked in and he grew into a very impressive man. At age 36, he is six feet three and a muscular 230 lbs. With his well-trimmed goatee, he has a definite resemblance to the home-run slugger Mark McGwire.

But Mario has more than a body, he has an aura of confidence. One never doubts that he is in command. He doesn't need to throw his weight around. You sense that he is in control.

"What is the worst thing that can happen to me?" he asks. "It is that someone attacks me physically." Nevertheless, he believes he can beat anyone. He doesn't show any insecurity because he doesn't feel any.

Another dimension of his aura is his voice, which is strong, reassuring and extremely pleasant. Mario learned how to use his voice during the 10 years he worked part-time as a karate teacher. He used his voice to teach the students how to expand and extend their physical powers. When he wanted students to kick, punch or move faster, he would raise his voice. When he wanted them to slow down, he lowered his voice. He developed his voice into an instrument of control.

While Mario was working nights teaching karate, he held a series of day jobs that allowed him to pay the rent and to observe how power is expressed in the suit-and-tie-wearing world. He recalls a marketing specialist who consulted with a company where he used to work. He was an odd-looking man with greasy hair and long fingernails. He made disgusting guttural and nasal noises when he spoke. Sometimes, he would raise his left hand over his head in order to scratch the right side of his face, which made him look like an orangutan. In meetings, he always laid six pencils on the table, and took notes with each in turn. He wore monogrammed shirts with someone else's initials on them.

This man was totally out of control. His appearance was careless and his every action signaled insecurity. Mario recalls that whenever he had to meet this man, he was unable to pay attention for the first 15 minutes. "I was shocked by his demeanor and his behavior," Mario says. "I couldn't follow his conversation. Many of us were trying to suppress our laughter during the meeting with him, and it was very hard to do." Mario, who was already thinking about a career coaching executives, says, "I decided my appearance is never going to be a distraction."

When he set out on his own, he was determined that his dress and grooming needed to reflect the confidence he feels, and show the edge that executives want. He didn't have a lot of money, but he traded some karate lessons for Hugo Boss suits and ties. He shopped carefully for the best shirts and shoes. And he invested in the most expensive eyeglasses, briefcase and haircut available. His clients notice that he is dressed as well as they are—and that he wears his clothes better. That helps convince them he has something to teach them.

"They feel the pressure of work and life," says Mario of his clients. "They are looking for something that can make them more noticeably effective." They are looking for an aura of confidence, like the one Mario developed for himself.

Putting your foot down

Spare room tycoons are frequently worried about where the next piece of business is coming from. As a result, we sometimes accept circumstances—such as very tight deadlines or difficult working conditions—that jeopardize our chances of delivering a top-quality product.

Confidence resides in being sure of what we can do. That implies that we also know what we *can't* do. While it's exciting to stretch our capabilities and master new fields, the confident spare room tycoon knows better than to promise the impossible. She tries instead to create circumstances that allow her to provide a high-quality result.

Ralf Graves learned this lesson almost by accident. At age 39, she was newly married, living in the UK, hanging around the house, and bored. For a dozen years, she had run her own interior design firm. She no longer liked the work, but she did like being in business for herself.

"I don't do housewife," she says. "Being a wife isn't bad, but being a housewife is not good."

She didn't know what to do, so she went to a temp agency to see what was available. She presented them with a formidable set of credentials: degrees in communication and education, experience running projects, ability to read construction documents. The agency found her a job with one of the contractors that was building the Channel Tunnel between the UK and France.

Ralf became involved in training some of the staff who would be working in the tunnel on the use of safety equipment. She had observed that the training being offered was adequate for making workers generally familiar with the equipment. She feared, however, that if the workers were actually called on to use the emergency equipment in a high-stress situation in the pitch-dark tunnel, they probably wouldn't survive.

Ralf was allowed to revamp the safety training completely, a job that she found extremely satisfying. Her problem was a boss who drove her crazy and expected her to clean up after his mistakes. When her contract was up, she left the job.

A short time later, she got a call from the contractor, who wanted her back. She didn't want to return to work for the contractor or the temp firm, she told them. Fine, came the reply, she could be an independent subcontractor. She didn't want to have to work with the bad boss, she added. No problem, came the response, he has already been fired. Then she asked for a large pay increase and a shorter work week, and all were accepted.

"I ran out of impossible demands," she said, so she took the work. It was her first independent project doing more or less what she had dreamed of doing when she was in college 20 years earlier. Moreover, it was a highly responsible position in one of the greatest construction projects ever.

"I worked so hard and enjoyed my work so much, I actually feel as if I dug some of the tunnel myself," Ralf says. That project gave her credibility to clients and, just as important, it gave her the confidence to put her foot down to make sure that the client gives her the time and resources to do an effective job.

Ralf is now based in the US, where she frequently works with internationally oriented professional organizations. Not long ago, a funding organization asked her to submit a proposal to train three female lawyers from Croatia. The goal was to have them come to the US to learn the logistics of human rights advocacy: how to run a non-profit organization, raise funds, do public relations, and lobby politicians.

Ralf was enthusiastic about the project, but as months passed with no response to her proposal, she became concerned. She also wanted to maintain a good relationship with the funder, with whom she would very likely be dealing again.

But the program she had proposed would take a lot of time to prepare, and it was already becoming too late to accomplish all she needed to do. She decided that it would be professional suicide to try to deliver a program without enough time to do it properly. She wrote the funding organization a polite, businesslike letter saying that she no longer wanted to be a candidate for this project. There was no longer enough time, she wrote, to do an excellent job. She was certain that if the funder went to anyone else to do the impossible, the competitor would inevitably turn in a poor performance. That might induce the funder both to manage their projects more efficiently, and to hire Ralf to carry them out.

"It's important to pull the plug sometimes," Ralf says. You need to be confident, however, that the time and money you demand for the project are fair and competitive. "You must make sure you're not bluffing," she adds.

Betting on yourself

One thing I've learned from talking to many different self-employed people and entrepreneurs is that the wisdom they expound is contradictory.

"Keep your costs low, don't expand too quickly or take on long-term commitments whose implications you can't foresee," goes one line of advice. (This one sounds a lot like me.)

"Seize the moment and opportunity," says the counter-argument. "If you pay attention to your fears and insecurities, you'll always be small. Make a bold move to become what you want to be."

Experienced independents will give you all sorts of advice, and though much of it is contradictory, none of it is wrong, at least for the people giving the advice. Other people, following the same advice, would very likely fail—especially if the advice is deeply at odds with their sense of themselves and the way they do things.

I'm afraid there's no way to know how many spare room tycoons succeed because they are conservative, how many succeed because they are bold, or how many fail for the same reasons. I think that it's good for careful people to be reminded that risk is often rewarded, and for those who follow their gut instincts to realize that systematic analysis can often lead to immensely profitable insight. But if you're not psychologically prepared, it's not wise to leap rashly into the unknown. You'll probably have a nasty fall. And when people who are addicted to adventure try to practice caution, they risk boring themselves to death.

"Be yourself" is probably the most useless piece of advice anyone can give. But if you are going into business for yourself, you had better know something about your strengths, and particularly your blind spots and your tolerance of risk.

Oddly, it was somebody I've known for years who made me aware of the very different styles of self-employment. Martha Hughes is a published writer of fiction, but she is also that rarest of animals, a liberal arts entrepreneur. She runs workshops to help people learn to write.

Everyone's career, indeed everyone's life, is something that is made up as we go along. I'm very aware of that. But as you can see from my previous tales, I tend to understand my story as a series of discoveries I have made and decisions I have taken, usually as a result of introspection. Martha, by contrast, jumps right in. Like a free jazz musician or an action painter, she believes that the learning comes only in the act of doing.

Martha's personal myth does not, therefore, involve internal struggles or promises made to God, but rather a succession of things she did without worrying too much about them. The key story she tells to explain her attitude concerns a trip she made to Europe after graduating from college. Her parents had always fantasized about travel, she says, but they never quite managed to go. Martha was determined to go, and to stay for a long time.

The day before she was to leave, her father asked her if she had enough money. She replied that she had $35. Shocked, he wrote her a check to make sure she wouldn't be impoverished the moment she landed. "But I would have gone if he hadn't given me the money," she says. And during the two years she traveled, she claims she became immune to the fear of not having enough money.

"I could be completely out of money and didn't die," she says. "I knew that something would always happen to save me." This lesson has stayed with her all her life. "If you have an education, you don't stop breathing because you don't have money. I have no fundamental anxiety about money."

Thus, a few years later when she had a job she loved but a boss she hated, she didn't hesitate to walk away from the good salary without any prospect of other income.

Martha's current business came about when, as part of a fellowship she had won, she was assigned to be a tutor at a summer school for aspiring writers. She decided that she could do better than this well-established program. So two months later, in 1991, she founded her company, Peripatetic Writing Workshop, and advertised for students. Six enrolled.

She rented an old Victorian house on an island in upstate New York. She was conference organizer, teacher, fiction tutor, seminar leader, trucker, cook, publicist and janitor all in one. (Trying to save money, she bought food and supplies in Mississippi and carried them north in a pickup truck that broke down, spilling toilet paper all over the interstate. It was a disaster then, but a good story now.)

Students were satisfied with this one-woman show, and word of mouth was good. She has continued her business, expanded, and brought in a partner and faculty members to help it grow. She has recently ventured overseas with conferences in Ireland, and she expects to continue to go global.

"If you have passion, and you look too closely at the danger, you'll never get to the passion," Martha insists. "Adventure means something to me. Winning means something to me. Curiosity means something to me. Being bored is the worst thing to me."

"In order to be an entrepreneur, you have to be a gambler," she advises. Martha obviously doesn't worry the way I do. So this advice works for her.

Serial entrepreneur

Marvin Schwam is a serial entrepreneur. He seems to have a new business about as often as some other people have a new suit. He has found many different ways to turn his artistic talents into products. Most, though not all, have worked. He has succeeded often enough that he is able to take the occasional failure in stride and move on to the next idea.

"The thought of going to work for someone else always terrifies me," Marvin says. "It has always been difficult for me to obey other people. Besides, I want to reap the rewards of my own risk taking."

He first went into business for himself at the age of 10. That's when his art teacher told him that he had a talent for making and painting ceramics. She let him use her kiln to fire them. It was his idea to sell them.

Most of Marvin's businesses have been animated by his desire to express his artistic creativity, combined with a knack for identifying opportunities and a willingness to take risks. In a series of businesses he has founded since childhood, he has been able to realize his artistic ideas on a large scale. And he has been able to make them pay. "I am very good at making things that nobody needs, but many people want," he says.

Marvin's first real business began when he was in high school. He made artificial flower arrangements, which he was able to have displayed in a local beauty salon, where they could be admired at length by the patrons. He was able to sell the arrangements first to the ladies under the hair dryers, and then to others. Soon, he found that he was making more money from this hobby than his father was earning from his job as a hardware salesman.

But Marvin realized that making floral arrangements for sale was a business with limited growth. He needed a way to profit from his talents on a larger scale. He knocked on the door of a company that imported artificial flowers and distributed hundreds of thousands of catalogues. He volunteered to go to the importer's factory two days a week without pay and create arrangements from the current selection of flowers and foliage. The importer would take pictures of his creations and pay a 2 percent commission on sales his arrangements generated.

At the age of 18, Marvin was earning as much as $2000 for each day of work he did, which was a very substantial amount four decades ago, and pretty impressive even today. This success gave Marvin confidence. "With my talents and creative abilities, I knew I could always find a way to make money."

Even so, after he graduated from college and was married, he felt that a man with a family to support ought to have a full-time job. He worked for a New York advertising agency for a couple of years but, dissatisfied, returned to artificial flowers. He worked briefly for a company that sold artificial arrangements for office building lobbies then, after that business was sold, started his own similar firm in 1968.

Marvin was able to place an elaborate indoor landscape in the lobby of a large office building, along with a sign advertising his company. An architect whose firm was in the building noticed it and got in touch with him. The firm was designing one of the first indoor regional shopping malls and needed to find something to enliven the interior. The mall had four wings, and the architect wondered if Marvin could design an indoor landscape based on the four seasons, featuring 60-foot trees. These would be ten times as tall as most artificial trees, four times as high as the biggest.

Only God can make a tree, the poem goes, but Marvin, ever the entrepreneur, decided to take a shot. He rented a loft and hired artisans, and delivered the design and the trees. The architects, the mall developers, and the shoppers all approved.

Marvin realized that the shopping mall was a new environment, and he had been the first to figure out how to decorate it. In 1970, he displayed his work and his successful project at a national shopping mall convention, and booked business from nine other malls. The following year, his firm did displays for 47 malls.

In 1981, Marvin came across a company that made mechanical Santa Clauses for display in department stores. The owner wanted to sell, and Marvin had an idea.

He bought the company, and scaled down the size and costumes of the animated figures from six feet to two. That way people could buy them for their own homes. He moved production to Taiwan to reduce the cost of making the figures, and suddenly what had been an item selling to only a handful of customers became a consumer product. In 1983, he sold $24 million worth of domestic-sized animated Santas, and the business was growing.

Marvin had once again created something unlikely, something people didn't know they wanted. But they did.

❖❖❖

Spare room tycoons must learn to be confident, and work at it regularly. That's not just because we want to feel good about ourselves. Self-worth can translate into net worth.

We often mistakenly assume that confidence is all in our heads. It's in our bodies too—in the way we move, stand, and speak. Our bodies express our inner state, but it's also possible to train the body to communicate confidence.

We must know what we're capable of doing, and know what risks we're comfortable taking. Sometimes it's good to try to expand these limits, but it's never wise to ignore them. That can ruin your sleep, threaten your sanity, and cause you to do a lousy job besides.

Some people—and they are always *other* people—seem to be born confident. The rest of us must work at it. That's all right. The results reward the effort. If we expect others to appreciate our worth, we must first do so ourselves.

6
You Are a Brand

It's not enough for the spare room tycoon to be a creator, a manager, a salesperson, and a strategist. You must also be a brand. You need to let others know that you exist, and that you stand for something meaningful.

Being a brand need not be as expensive as it sounds, however, because we already have a head start. Independents can often establish our brands as effectively through our presentation and behavior as through costly advertising or public relations.

Large corporations devote a great deal of care, time and money to formulating and projecting an identity. At a time when giants seem to be swallowing even larger giants daily, these business entities try to convince us that they have the qualities that we would expect to find in individuals; indeed, in our friends.

Thus, they take pains to establish a particular character. Many insurance companies, for example, seek to impress us with their old-money rectitude and conservatism. Disney evokes the memory of its founder Walt, and the many characters the company has created, from

Mickey Mouse to the Lion King. Volvo has even been able to capitalize on the pessimism that seems endemic to Swedes. Automobile accidents are inevitable, the company tells us, and we work obsessively to be sure that you survive them.

Many companies exploit a myth of their origins. Apple Computer, for example, trades on its entrepreneurial origins in a garage, and presents itself as the computer company that takes interesting, exciting chances. For years, an actor playing Charles Merrill, founder of Merrill Lynch, harangued the viewing public with common sense; and even the ambiguous figure of Henry Ford, seen by some as a hateful genius, has been expensively celebrated for realizing the dream of a car for the masses.

Millions have been spent on such campaigns, and what is their purpose? It is to make giant businesses seem more like individual people. It is to give these companies a personality, perhaps even a soul.

Guess what? We spare room tycoons *are* individuals. We do possess character. We have personalities. And each of us is more soulful than Unilever, Exxon, Coca-Cola or Nestlé, any day of the week. Our businesses embody our real identities, not artificial ones.

It is important for those of us who are in business for ourselves to have a strong sense of who we are. For the most part, I think we do. Nearly everyone with whom I spoke saw their business as an outgrowth of their own talents, their own interests, their own values, their own commitments. While we need to refrain from identifying too completely with our businesses, we do see our businesses as, at least, a reflection of our identities. This sense that we have of ourselves can give our businesses an integrity that bigger companies can only envy.

What the giants have that we don't, however, is the ability to project their identity in the world. They can conduct massive advertising campaigns. Few of us can do the same. (One spare room tycoon I spoke with stopped advertising when he realized that he was doing it simply to assuage his own ego, and make his friends view him as successful. He decided that it's cheaper and more enjoyable to take his friends out to dinner.)

We do have ways of projecting our identity, nevertheless, and they are very important. Our clothes, our letterhead, our manners, the professionalism of our behavior, and the care with which we clean up after are all ways of projecting a positive identity in the world.

The other way we express our identity is by joining together, by volunteering and becoming known to large numbers of people. We may be on our own, but nearly all of us belong to several different communities: our neighborhoods, our industries, people who share our problems, our interests or our pleasures. We discover and express who we are when we interact with other people. And who knows, some of them may turn out to be customers.

A myth of my own

I have my own founding myth. It predates my decision to go into business for myself by several years. But it remains the bedrock of my career. It is a wellspring of my passion and my enterprise, the ultimate explanation of all I have done.

It took place when I was engaged in what I believed to be a struggle for survival. After finishing my bachelor's degree at the University of Hong Kong, I moved to the US and earned degrees at the University of Chicago and the University of Michigan. I had decided that I wanted to spend the rest of my life in the US. The problem was that my visas had expired, and I was supposed to leave. When I didn't go, I became, officially, an illegal alien.

I knew others in my situation who got around the problem by entering into fictitious marriages. I didn't want to do that. I was determined to be legal and above board, and I spent $20,000—more money than I had—on fees to a lawyer to figure out how. After running up his charges, he told me that my situation was, essentially, hopeless. Meanwhile, China was opening itself to business from the West, and several large companies offered me jobs. They withdrew the offers when they learned of my immigration status. I felt as if a golden opportunity was opening to me, and at the same time being snatched away.

I borrowed some money from friends and an uncle. Another friend gave me food, a place to stay, and emotional support. I sat in his apartment day after day and typed up more than 1000 job application letters until the typewriter broke.

One day, near despair, I walked into Philadelphia's Cathedral of Saints Peter and Paul. I'm not a Catholic. I'm not even a Christian. I don't really know what to do in a church. But that somber, lofty, baroque-style edifice seemed to be a place where I needed to be.

I knelt in the pew and silently addressed God. "If you can let me stay in this country legally," I proposed. "I

promise to help pull China and America closer together."
(I figured that this was something God would want my
help on, though I can't tell you exactly why.)

Later, I found out that I was doing what psycholo-
gists call "bargaining," and that it's a stage people go
through on the road to accepting the death of a loved one
or a cherished dream. It's assumed to be futile, some even
think it is self-destructive. Fortunately, I didn't know that
then.

What my bargaining did was make me look deep
within myself to find something of great importance to
which I was singularly equipped to make a contribution.
I found a reason for me to be on this earth. I had discovered a story of which I could be the hero. I had forged my
own myth.

Not long after, my prayer was answered. Some
would argue that it was because I found a highly skilled
lawyer who was committed to my case. I don't presume,
however, to know the means by which God might realize
His will.

As my fortunes changed, I realized that I would not
have promised God to do something I really didn't want
to do. In a troubled moment, I discovered a vocation, an
identity, a reason for my existence, a focus for my energy.

I think those of us who work on our own must have
our own personal myths, visions of our lives as we would
like to live them, visions of the world as we would like to
leave it.

And if you make a vow, as I did, you keep it. We
should keep such vows because they define the core of
our being—the things that set us apart from those who
are just in it for the money.

By the way, I rarely tell prospects or clients about my myth, although they do understand its essence. Just the other day, in the midst of a discussion of business details, a client alluded to my project of pulling China and America closer together. I don't recall ever telling her directly that that's what I'm doing. But by embodying a larger ideal, I increase the respect that clients feel for me. I couldn't ask anyone else to do that for me. It is a personal brand, perhaps, but it is also who I am.

A strong identity

This is a tale of temptation. It is about one of those rare people who knew, almost from birth, that he would live by following his own vision. One could say that it is about the affirmation of identity, but in fact, Sam Maitin's identity was so firmly rooted he scarcely had to think about it.

Sam is an artist. He believes that being independent is an essential part of being an artist. He had his last full-time job when he was a teenager. Now he is in his seventies. He has worried about what he should paint, or whether he should take a particular commission, but he has never had to worry about who he is.

Sam says he made his choice to be independent and an artist once and for all when he was a young man, recently out of school. In order to make a living, he was doing freelance graphic work for magazines and advertising agencies, and he found that he was very good at it. However, he viewed these assignments as expedients to put food on the table and pay the bills. They were not what he wanted to spend his life doing.

He was, nevertheless, pleased when he was summoned to the office of Herbert Lubalin, who was quickly establishing himself as one of the most influential graphic designers in the world. Sam respected Lubalin's design work, and he was hoping to get some commissions from his firm. But this was not what Lubalin had in mind.

Lubalin began by praising Sam and saying he could contribute a lot to his company. He then offered him a full-time job, with a wage that was several times his annual earnings. It was, for Sam, an almost unimaginable sum. But it seemed to require him to live a kind of life he had never aspired to, to become another kind of person.

He told Lubalin that while he wanted to work for him, he was not looking for a full-time job, that he wanted to be an artist. Lubalin's reply was to increase his offer by about 25 percent. "Is that good enough?" he asked.

Sam was shocked. He has never in his life been a good negotiator, and he wasn't trying to negotiate at that moment. Nevertheless, he was pleasantly surprised by how well he was doing at it. But what surprised him most was that Lubalin seemed unable to take his aspiration seriously. For Lubalin, the expressed desire to be an independent artist was merely a negotiating ploy; for Sam it was an identity. He said no again.

Lubalin told Sam to wait for a moment as he left the office. He returned with the owner of the firm. "OK," said the owner. "This will be our final offer. We don't want to negotiate with you any more." Then he quoted a sum that was nearly twice the original, very high figure.

Sam said no yet again. The owner stared at him long and hard and walked out.

Then he asked Lubalin whether he could get any

freelance assignments from the firm. Lubalin replied that he could not.

It hadn't really occurred to Sam that he could have done anything but what he did. Those to whom he told the story immediately afterward disagreed. They thought he had been foolish, even suicidal, to walk away from such an opportunity. One artist friend argued that if he stayed for two years, he would earn as much as he might in twenty doing what he was doing. Then he could afford to pursue his art.

"Besides," the friend added, "if you worked there, you could hire me to freelance."

In the years since, Sam admits that he has felt a twinge or two of regret for walking away from all that money. But at the moment it happened, he recalls, he felt scarcely any doubt. He was acting on something that he had always known: He had to be independent. He is an artist. That is his identity.

Dressed to bill

I am not an extravagant person. You might even say I'm borderline stingy. But one area where I don't economize is in the quality, cut, and fit of the clothes I wear. Over the years I have been in business, I have become more and more convinced that the image that independent business people project to their customers, potential customers and the world at large is absolutely crucial.

Dressing well communicates that you have respect for yourself and for those with whom you do business. It tells people that you are attentive to detail. It encourages them to pay more attention to what you are saying. You feel better about what you say and do when you feel you look good. You smile more comfortably. You speak with authority. Clothes don't guarantee success, but when you are the business, you need every edge you can find.

When I was about to start my business, I used one of my last paychecks to buy the most expensive suit I had ever owned, along with a costly cashmere overcoat. New clothes symbolize a new life, which is why most people change their wardrobes when they change jobs or go independent.

When I wore these clothes to the office building where I worked, I felt that I gave off an aura I didn't feel on ordinary work days. As I entered the elevator, a fellow passenger—someone I'd never seen before in my life— looked at me and exclaimed, "Wow, look at that suit!" That unsolicited endorsement gave me a jolt of confidence. I felt, irrationally perhaps, that I was going to be able to make it in business on my own.

As I thought about that incident, I realized that I would never have bought such a suit if I had viewed it, as my soon-to-be-former co-workers did, as a uniform that revealed their adherence to the standards of a large organization. Rather, this suit was intended to project that I am an extraordinary person with something of great value to offer. Most people dress to belong. The spare room tycoon must dress to bill.

Not long ago, there was a television advertisement for office supplies whose message was that home-based professionals need never change out of their fuzzy bunny slippers. This expressed a dangerous stereotype that is tinged with envy. Many people assume that because those who work at home are free from the structures of corporate life, they are not fully professional. It is assumed that we're not working a full day, that we sleep late and loll about in pajamas. "I hope I didn't wake you," one client began a conversation, when he called not very early one morning.

It's true that I don't dress the same way when I know I won't be leaving the house as I do when I see a client. (One reason my suits look good is that I don't wear them every day.) But when I leave my office, I am aware that I must overcome the bunny slippers stereotype, and embody professionalism through my wardrobe, carriage and demeanor.

The power of clothing can often be observed most strongly when others' minds wander. When a client's or prospect's attention begins to flag during a meeting or presentation, they often fix on something you are wearing or carrying. I recall a CEO ogling my briefcase as we waited in the airport in Shanghai, a woman executive who stared at my shoes, and another women who praised my eyeglasses.

You'd really prefer that people listened intently and ceaselessly to what you say. But you do want to impress them favorably in every way. If they end the meeting wanting a piece of you, that's (usually) a good thing.

Looking good on paper

One of the first things you have to do when you go into business for yourself is to get your own business cards, letterheads and envelopes. Many people make a mistake when they do this. They think that they are simply purchasing office supplies. What you're really doing is creating a brand for your business, one that is often the only image many people will ever see.

It's just as important for you to have a corporate identity as it is for IBM. It may even be more important because while IBM is a familiar brand, few people know who you are. Self-employed people are often viewed as being between jobs. If your stationery and your business card have an improvised, stopgap look, you will merely confirm that stereotype.

It's easy, nowadays, to sit at your computer and come up with something that looks more or less all right. It is very difficult, though, to quickly improvise something that communicates the substance of what you do, the emotional tone that you bring to the job, and the seriousness of your intent. But that's exactly what your letterhead and your business card ought to do.

I started in business with good-looking stationery. It was designed for me by a very talented former assistant. It featured a logo with the letter *i* in lower case in a typeface that, to me, evoked the brushstroke of Chinese calligraphy. (It had a bit of the feel of Lucent Technology's brushstroke circle.) For me, the letter was the subtlest possible allusion to my Asian specialty, and it stood for "idea."

I liked the design, and very impetuously had a great quantity of it printed. I ignored a friend who argued that nobody else would possibly be able to figure out what I was trying to say. When a prospective client asked me what the *i* stood for, I began to realize that while my identity was more than respectable, it was ambiguous, and certainly not compelling. Later, I noticed that an italic *i* that resembled my logo is used internationally as an international symbol for information. My firm wasn't in the business of telling people where to get the bus from the airport to downtown. I needed a logo that couldn't possibly be confused with anything so mundane.

My next brand identity was based on the first, but it was homemade. I replaced the old logo with my chop—stylized versions of the three Chinese characters that made up my name, inside a square border. Such chops, or inked stamps, are a familiar feature of Chinese culture, often replacing a signature. I had substituted an ambiguous identity with my own. But while my previous stationery was a harmonious design, my new one looked like the improvisation it was. I kept using this stationery as my business declined. I knew it wasn't good, but I didn't want to make the investment to change it.

Finally, in 1991, I came up with a new name for my business, Asia Marketing and Management, and I asked Steve Ong, a good friend who has worked as an art director for several top advertising agencies, to design my identity. I thought he would just go away and come up with something, but instead, he asked me some difficult questions. What was my business about? What did I aspire to do? What did I want to communicate?

Even though Steve knew me well, he probed and looked for clues about the messages—beyond my name, title, address and telephone number—that I needed my letterhead and business card to express. We spent most of an evening discussing this. I remember telling him that I wanted to run a business that would help pull two continents together, like Hercules.

What he came back with was a design that was so

shockingly strong, I almost rejected it. I had figured I would get rid of the chop, but he came back with it larger, and in red. I realized that what had been wrong with my chop on the old letterhead was that it was too small; it almost seemed to be apologizing for my involvement in Asia. Then he stacked the first letters of my company name, *AMM*, vertically. It reminded me of Giotto's bell tower in Florence. I knew that most people wouldn't see that, but the square and diagonal forms do evoke a solid structure, something I wanted people to perceive. This design is most assertive on the business card, which is vertical, not horizontal.

I went ahead with the design, though I wasn't used to being quite so formidable. I worried that it might be a bit much. Then one day, I was talking with a partner of an enormous law firm. "You know," he said, unprompted, "your stationery is much better than ours." I realized at that moment that my brand identity needs to be stronger and more sophisticated than that of a larger, more established firm. I'm independent, and I need to be recognized. My business card comes on strong, and so do I.

How not to network

Network! Network! Network!

That's an imperative that appears in just about every book about self-employment. And it's advice that spare room tycoons give each other and try to follow themselves. It's good advice as far as it goes. Getting out and getting to know people is one of the best ways to become known. Yet this dictum can lead as often to wheel spinning and time wasting as to lasting, useful relationships.

Networking works only if you keep in mind how others will benefit.

I recently had an encounter with someone who is clearly working hard at networking, but getting it all wrong. We met after a meeting of independent professionals, the sort of group that's probably more useful for camaraderie and commiseration than making business contacts. He told me that he had just left a large company, and was now working as a consultant doing marketing and strategic planning.

Within the first few seconds of our conversation, I could tell that he didn't care to interact with me as another human being, or even as a professional colleague. I was a networking target. He wanted to know everything about the way I did business and who my clients were. He didn't want to tell me a thing about himself. As we spoke, I felt he was a mosquito, drawing blood before moving on to his next prey.

A few days later, I received a personal note from him following up on our contact. This is what all the books advise, and it's not a bad idea if you really feel that some rapport was established. But when I read the salutation, "Dear Bill," any thought I might have had of communicating further with him vanished. The minimum requirement for a personal note is to get the person's name right.

The letter said he was glad to have met me, that he wanted to get new business through me and that he might be able to pass new business to me. I think that this is unlikely, given that I don't have a clear idea of either what he does or who he is, and he had shown little real interest in me.

A few days later he telephoned me. He said he

wanted to know the secret of my staying power. I was willing to talk, but he still wouldn't tell me a thing about what he was trying to do. He had sent me a brochure that said he held an MBA from Harvard, but I had little sense of him as a person. I wanted to get off the telephone, but I did feel a certain pity for his cluelessness. Then, as I was in mid-sentence, he told me that there was another call he had to take, and that he'd get back to me. I was relieved. I didn't expect to hear from him again, and I was right.

This sort of behavior is stupid, but all too common. He is probably repeating his mistakes and wondering why he's not getting anywhere.

Being in business for yourself is an activity that feeds obsession. While developing your business is the most important thing in your life, it isn't the most important thing in anybody else's life.

That means that you should not be a predatory networker, focused only on how other people can help you. Others can spot that attitude and back away from it fast. They don't want to waste their networking time with someone who is not going to listen.

Other people have their own preoccupations and obsessions, many of them quite interesting, instructive and possibly even profitable. The only way that networking can possibly work is if you can show others that you can offer them ways to solve their problems and improve their lives. The first step in doing so is paying real attention to what people say.

I often think that the very term networking confuses and misleads people who try to do it. Networking sounds like something cold and efficient, very different from the often slow and indeterminate acts of meeting new people, finding mutual interests and activities and, at least to some extent, opening up to them emotionally.

One of my clients once asked a Chinese executive whom we were visiting how to do successful business in China. The executive replied, "Make friends first." This was frustrating advice, because most business people don't have the time, patience or interest to follow it, particularly when they are dealing with people they perceive as very different from themselves.

Nevertheless, this is advice that works as well in Seattle, Sydney, or Stockholm as it does in Shanghai. Friendships are risky and open ended. You cannot tell where they will lead, and that's what's good about them. The uncertainty is mostly on the upside.

It's true that you can do good business with people that you don't like, so long as one of you offers something the other needs. Networking, though, is something different. It's really an exploration of other people, and its payoff is more likely to come later than sooner.

Dealing with those you meet as real people rather than networking targets might seem time consuming, but it is far more likely to produce good results. And it's much more fun.

Winning recognition

One of the toughest parts of starting in business is what might be called the "who the hell are you?" factor.

It's not so much that anyone actually asks you that rude question (though you might sometimes ask it of yourself). More often, you detect this attitude in a brusque, impatient response from someone you meet, or the suspicion that you're being ignored because someone important is nearby.

One common response to this problem is to open an impressive office. That was Alan Kaplan's instinct when, at the age of 32, after a year of research and preparation, he set off on his own as a recruiter of highly paid executives and technical staff. Fortunately, though, he sought advice from seasoned people who warned him of the danger of taking on so much overhead at the outset.

And when he ended up starting the business in his townhouse, he was in the right place at the right time. "It was starting to become acceptable to be a virtual company," he said, and as he became more involved in technology fields, he found that clients envied his work situation.

Nevertheless, he still faced the problem of establishing a real business profile from his home office. His solution was to become a volunteer.

I met Alan because he has held many offices in the Entrepreneurs' Forum of Greater Philadelphia. And that's probably how most people have met him. His leadership in this group has provided him with an opportunity to become known and to show influential people what he can do.

"Starting as a one-man firm, all you have is your personality and integrity," says Alan. He began to look around for ways to have an impact and become better known. Many business and professional groups are voluntary organizations that are always looking for new blood and new energy to keep their programs going. A newcomer can rise quickly.

Alan saw a newspaper article about the Entrepreneurs' Forum a few months after he started his business, and decided to call the person quoted in the article. When this contact called him back, he said the organization's most important immediate goal was to find more corporate sponsorship to expand the scope and programming of the forum.

Alan got on the telephone. Because he was working for the forum, and not for himself, he was able confidently to call, and get through, to powerful people who might have ducked a cold call from a newly minted recruiter. He quickly rounded up half a dozen new sponsors, who provided enough money to double the organization's budget. Anyone who pulls off a coup like that will be asked to do more. Naturally, Alan was.

Alan has since held numerous offices in the forum, including president. In these roles, he has built relationships with corporate executives, lawyers and others who are in a position to use or recommend his services. He doesn't market directly in this way, but people most often do business with those they know.

"I go to every meeting," Alan says. "I take time to talk to people, to make a contribution. I help people when there is an opportunity to help them. Consistency is critical. It is like brand recognition. People know that you've been there."

Alan is also very careful to follow up contacts. "Every person that I meet will get a thank you note within 24 hours after our meeting. This makes people feel that I am professional and responsive. Follow-up is so simple; it's the most basic thing. But most people don't do it."

What Alan is doing is, you might say, nothing but networking. This is true, but it is networking for the long haul. He devotes a lot of time and energy to the forum, even when it is not evident that his efforts will soon contribute to his bottom line. He is not a hit-and-run networker. He works with other people on common projects for long periods of time. That's the only way to establish the image of consistency, reliability and effectiveness that he is looking for.

Few people have to ask who the hell Alan is. By taking a leadership role in the forum, he became its president. But more importantly, he became a figure in the community.

❖❖❖

A brand is a distillation of identity and an affirmation of quality. Big companies use brands to give their products attributes that most spare room tycoons already possess.

The most essential part of brand identity comes from within. It consists of purpose, conviction and commitment. Other aspects—such as the way you dress, the briefcase you carry, the business card you pass out— might seem superficial. But they only work when they serve as outward signs of your mission and your commitment to quality.

How you behave among other people is also an essential part of your brand. Being known as a person who cares about others adds to the value of your products and services. If you can make people trust you,

you have succeeded in doing what large corporations spend millions to achieve for their brands.

7
Setting a Price

"How much should I charge?" This is a question that all spare room tycoons will ask till the day they die. If you feel lost, you're not alone. Huge training industries have grown up just to help people learn how to price—from huge multinationals to people like us.

But this is no cause for concern. Part of pricing is a science. The rest is confidence in action. You must begin with a solid estimate of all your business costs, and a well-founded idea of how much you need to support yourself. While there are wide variations in pricing practices from industry to industry, it will be worth your time to research your field and see what competitors are charging.

Because we usually have lower fixed expenses, spare room tycoons can often prosper at a lower price point than our larger competitors. Often, though, we offer benefits that nobody else can provide, and we should be sure to point this out to potential customers, and to charge for the added value we provide.

There is, however, one iron rule of pricing: You must charge enough to live.

When I started my business, I bought a book that offered a formula. It said that you should set your hourly rate at a level that would give you a reasonable living if you are able to sell about one third of your available hours. Another third of your time should be allocated to finding new business. The last third is taken up with such activities as bookkeeping, walking to the post office, gnashing your teeth and checking your email. I found this very useful advice because I was able to make it work. It helped me keep in mind how much time I need to spend promoting.

There are other formulas that apply to retailing, manufacturing or other sorts of services, and most of them are helpful both because they stress how much of an entrepreneur's time is spent doing apparently nonproductive work, and because they offer a discipline that many who are new to business sorely need.

None of these formulas work, however, if you don't offer what buyers want at the rates you need to charge to stay in business. All too often, beginners think that they can undercharge in order to get business. This seems like a logical tactic, but it's the road to ruin. It costs money and may make it difficult to sustain your business. It can lead some customers to wonder whether you really know what you're doing. And it can distract you from the more difficult, but perhaps more rewarding, task of finding something you can offer at a price that gives you a good income.

Nevertheless, just about every self-employed person I know has adopted this tactic at least once.

I did it during the late 1980s when things were looking particularly gloomy in China. I decided to offer a one-day seminar for a very low price, essentially in the hope of getting my foot in the door. All I need, I told myself, is to find one big company that's interested.

I spent thousands of dollars on printing, postage and mailing list rentals. The phone rang only a few times, and I sold just one seminar. I was encouraged, however, because this company was a world leader in a technology that China desperately needed. And it was relatively nearby, which usually helps.

After the seminar, there was even a small follow-up consulting assignment. I didn't dare charge very much for it because I didn't want to scare a potentially lucrative client away. Later I found out that, in the two years after my seminar, the company made more than $1 million in sales in China. Yet I had charged only a few thousand dollars, merely enough to pay for my mailing campaign. That meant that I had done several months of work, and offered valuable counsel, without making any money at all. I had not respected the value of what I was offering to this company. How could I expect the client to do so?

Soon after, this company was sold, and it did not, in the end, become a long-term customer. But if it had, I might have had difficulty raising my rates. You need to establish your price from the very beginning, or you will always be at a disadvantage.

If you charge too little, you could find yourself working full-time for less than it costs you to survive. Then, if you lose even a little piece of business, the results can be disastrous. Soon you'll be looking at the want ads seeking to serve the corporate kingdoms once more. The samurai is killed by his own cheap sword.

Getting what you're worth

When I first started as an independent, I wasn't merely happy when I got new business. I was amazed! I remember literally jumping up and down with joy when people decided they needed me, or, more accurately, my services. I was also relieved because I needed the income.

It's probably not surprising, given my state of mind, that I was undercharging. I had no experience running my own business. And although I was living in a fairly impressive apartment, my needs were modest. I based my rates on my immediate needs. I didn't dare think that my charges should reflect the full value I brought to the company that needed my services, probably because I feared that there wasn't any.

In the years since then, I have found that the key issue in whether you will get the job is not the fee, but rather your ability to outline a convincing course of action that promises a good outcome. In most projects, the difference between success and failure is going to be much larger than your fee.

You get business because others come to you with a need to be addressed. If you can meet the need, they will pay. If they don't want what you can do, you can cut your fees to nothing and still never get work.

In the years I have been in business, I have come in contact with many companies that I firmly believe need my services. Nevertheless, my belief doesn't count. A barber can stand on the street and look at all the people passing by who need haircuts. If he cuts the price to try to make them walk in the door, passersby might think

"What a cheap barber"—but they won't walk in the door if they don't think they need a haircut.

Likewise, I have had clients who have come out of the blue and used my services. I have learned, very slowly, that I can't predict who will decide to need me, or when. All I can do is make sure I charge fairly—both for my client and myself—when they do. This is easier to do, of course, when you have enough business coming in so that no particular job seems a matter of life or death.

Still, standing by your price is good discipline, in good times or bad. Most of the time it works, but it takes courage.

Not long ago, I did a small amount of work for one of those companies I previously decided should be using my services. The results were excellent, and I was pleased to receive a call asking me to discuss a much larger project. It would require many months of hard work, and involve a trip to China with a top executive.

I was able to put together a sound proposal very quickly, then I began to agonize over the price. I hoped that my work for this client would go beyond this project, substantial as it was. It would be valuable to have so much time with the executive who would decide whether to use my services in the future. These are all things I have used in the past as excuses to undercharge. This time was different.

I quoted a price that was, I think, reasonable, but somewhat more than I have charged long-standing clients. Two weeks later, the phone rang, and it was the executive with whom I would be traveling.

"We would like to go ahead with this proposal," she said. "But is your fee rigid?" In the past, I had rarely come to this point. I had undercharged from the start. But I summoned my courage.

"Please don't take this the wrong way," I replied. "I don't want to be rigid. If you were to insist that I take 10 percent off my fee, I might consider going ahead with the project anyway. On the other hand, I don't want to feel resentful when I do the work."

"OK," she replied. "Let's just get started." A few minutes later she faxed me the contract, and the first payment arrived the next day.

This conversation took less than a minute. During that time I told someone whose work I deeply wanted to win that I wanted to be paid fairly, if she didn't mind. She didn't mind at all! We had a wonderful trip to China. She was extremely happy with the results of my work.

I'd like to tell you that her company is an ongoing client, though at the moment, at least, that is not the case. Shortly after we returned, the company went through a corporate merger, and the executive with whom I traveled is no longer responsible for Asia. Perhaps I'll get the client back some day, but it is not a sure thing.

Even so, this less than perfect ending makes my point even stronger. If I had undercharged to get the client, I would still have been out of luck when the shakeup came. As it was, I did a good job for the company when it felt it needed me. I was paid well for it. And I have nothing to regret.

Prices and values

Setting prices that really reflect the value of your services takes discipline and courage. And as Fran McElroy, who

runs a video production firm, has discovered, the toughest people to charge are often those you admire the most.

Fran went independent after two distinct careers.
The first was as a staffer for Senator Edward Kennedy,
which she recalls as a time of idealism and youthful
enthusiasm. The second was as a program developer for a
public television station, where, she feels, her anti-author-
itarian attitude made her a prime candidate for downsizing.

When she set up her business, her goal was, in a
sense, to combine her liberal political philosophy with
the skills that she had acquired in television. She incor-
porated her business as a nonprofit. Its intent is to serve
other nonprofit organizations, particularly charities and
cultural institutions, by making educational films,
fundraising videos, public service announcements, and
documentary films.

Television and film production is expensive by
nature, and Fran is very proud of the results she has
achieved on tiny budgets. "They have no money, yet they
want all the bells and whistles," she says of her nonprofit
clients, "and often I'm able to oblige." One way she does
this is by convincing her contractors and suppliers of the
worthiness of the cause so that they are willing to settle
for lower fees than they usually charge. The other way she
does it is pay herself next to nothing.

"It's just my liberal guilt," Fran says. "Something
inside tells me that I shouldn't take money from organizations that serve the homebound elderly and the
homeless."

Recently, after one of her videos won a national
award from an association of philanthropists, Fran real-

ized that she was placing too low a value on what she does—not only in the prices she quotes, but in the way she thinks about her work. In imagining that she was taking food from the mouths of the homeless, she was forgetting that her videos serve the organizations for which she works and, by assisting their public awareness and fundraising, help to keep them in business.

"Any charity has to find the money to get its message out," she says. As a consequence, she has decided that she has to charge enough to ensure the future of her own business. Fran doesn't intend to gouge the poor, merely to compensate herself fairly.

She recently made a proposal whose costs reflected this new, realistic attitude. "They said yes, and I was absolutely shocked," says Fran. "I'm learning."

Like Fran, most spare room tycoons grapple daily with the tangled issues of pricing and self-esteem. And her dilemma demonstrates that having admirable, even saintly, customers—a problem most of us don't face—doesn't make running your business any easier.

Calculating how to charge

As the preceding stories have suggested, pricing is a very emotional issue. But it is not just confidence in action. It is best if you can base your prices on solid data, or, failing that, reasonable, easily explained assumptions. That way, if a prospect challenges your prices, you can answer rationally, rather than view it as an attack on your competency or worth as a person.

See it for a moment from your prospective client's point of view. Nobody likes to overpay. Everyone wants

value, which rests on meeting clearly defined expectations. Everyone understands that a fine restaurant cannot
sell its food at McDonald's prices, and it's equally true
that nobody wants to pay a high price for food of
McDonald's quality. Yet both the fine restaurant and the
fast-food restaurant can succeed at meeting the different
expectations the customer brings to them. Both can offer
good value.

It's difficult to set a formula for how to charge. It
depends on what you offer, who your competition is and
the unique circumstances of you and your client at a particular moment. Obviously you want to know what others
are charging, and you also want to be able to point out the
unique attributes of what you offer, so that the customer
will know enough to value it more.

My friend Rick Schilling, whom we met earlier,
places banking professionals in temporary jobs. It is
important for him to have a solid, quantitative justifica-
tion both for the salaries he pays to those he places and
for the prices he charges his clients. He believes that he
does best for everyone when he lays all the data out on
the table.

He tells a prospective client how much he expects to
pay the contractor on a particular job, and how much he
needs in addition to run his business and make a profit.
He also makes sure they know that an important part of
the value of his fee is quality control—double-checking
references, for example, so that he can guarantee that
anyone he sends out will be able to do the job specified.

Recently, an accounting firm called Rick searching
for a financial professional with expertise in assessing the
value of a business. One of the accounting firm's clients

wanted to sell his business, and asked the firm to submit an evaluation report. The firm did not have anyone who could do the job, or even learn to do so in a cost-effective way.

Moreover, the job was urgent. The firm needed someone who could do the job without close supervision, and get going immediately. Rick was able quickly to identify a banker in his database who had specialized in such valuations.

Rick told the accountants that he would bill $75 an hour for the banker's time. Of this fee, $50 an hour would be paid to the banker and the rest would cover his service. He calculated his payment to the banker by determining that a full-time employee with that experience would make about $80,000 a year, plus health, vacation, retirement and other fringe benefits equivalent to about 30 percent more. This translates to roughly $50 an hour.

Rick had discussed the $50 rate with the banker, who had accepted it. Rick also disclosed what he would be charging. Sometimes, he says, potential contractors are willing to accept less than the fee he calculates, but he doesn't allow them to do it.

He then got in touch with the accounting firm and quoted the price he would charge. The person with whom he spoke didn't object to the price, so Rick went ahead and faxed the candidate's resumé.

That's when the negotiation hit a snag. The accountants called back and said that their budget only allowed expenditure of $38 an hour total, to be divided between the banker and Rick.

Rick felt that the accountants shouldn't be negotiating at this point because he had told them the rate he would charge before he faxed the resumé. But he didn't vent his displeasure. He merely informed the accountants that, for $38, they would only be able to engage someone of lower expertise and experience. He gave them the name of a large temporary staffing agency that specialized in providing help at that price point. Very politely, and in a helpful manner, Rick was telling the accountants that he was not accepting their fee, nor was he willing to haggle.

His cool demeanor was based on absolute certainty that the accountants couldn't find the professional they needed at that price. Two days later, the accountants called back, and Rick suggested that they meet.

Rick was surprised that the accountants were willing to show the same openness about their fee structure that Rick had. Why they did so is somewhat of a mystery, because it surely didn't bolster their case. Their pay scale began at $250 an hour for a partner's time, $150 for an associate partner, and so on down the line. Because Rick's banker was providing a highly specialized form of expertise, most of his time could probably be billed at the highest rate. Indeed, the firm had no partners who could do the job.

Rick also sensed that the accountant's client was beginning to feel impatient. He felt no need to compromise, because his fees had a sound basis and the accountants were not able to do better elsewhere. The meeting ended with agreement by the accountants to pay Rick $75, the fee he had originally quoted.

Rick was also careful to ensure that the fee would be paid in a timely way. "Getting the business doesn't mean you'll get paid," he said, adding that law, accounting and other professional firms have a generally poor reputation for paying on time.

He drew up a letter of agreement specifying that he could be paid weekly, within seven days of receipt of the invoice. The letter also specified a financial penalty, payable to Rick, if the firm decided to hire the professional full time. This letter of agreement was an enforceable legal contract.

Rick's professional did his job well, and the accountants and their client were happy. This transaction led to more, less contentious, assignments from the firm.

By being calculating, and open about his calculations, Rick kept emotions out of the negotiation. And that's how he got his price.

Businesslike billing

Nearly all spare room tycoons sometimes worry about how much to bill. Many don't think *enough* about how to bill. They are careless about payment arrangements in their work agreements. They are slow to bill. And they send invoices that aren't sufficiently specific about the terms of payment.

This sort of conduct is understandable. People are often shy about asking for payment, particularly if they don't know whether the customer is satisfied with what they have provided. But it can also be self-destructive. Most companies don't pay bills any faster than they need to. Your billing must be timely and clear, or else you will spend your life in a cashflow squeeze.

The best opportunity to deal with payment issues is at the very beginning of your relationship with the client.

Practices vary from business to business, but as a general rule, you should not begin work or provide products without a purchase order, an agreement signed by an authorized representative of your customer, or some other form of legally binding contract.

Everyone understands that such a letter must specify how much you will be paid, but many people become careless about specifying *when* it will be paid. This is a matter for negotiation that ought to be handled up front.

If you go ahead with just a verbal understanding or a handshake, you will often find that a contract must still be executed once you have finished, and that this can be time consuming.

One of my friends agreed, on a verbal basis, to do a small but very urgent job for an arm of Microsoft. A week or so after he was done, he sent an invoice. Several weeks later, he received not a check, but a thick packet from Microsoft. A letter explained that his invoice could not be processed because he was not a registered vendor, and most of the rest of the packet consisted of forms to be filled out to attain that status. There was also a sheet specifying a precise format for all invoices.

The forms, which were designed for large companies not one-person operations, were forbidding but not onerous. They did, however, require him to give Microsoft sixty days to pay, following the receipt of an appropriate invoice from a registered vendor. Nearly two months had already gone by. He realized that Microsoft would be paying him about four months after the rush assignment, and would still be, by its own definition, on time. If he had addressed this issue at the beginning, he could probably have received payment at least two months sooner.

When I agree to do a project, I almost always ask for some of the money to be paid before I will begin the project. This requirement, which few clients have ever argued with, assures me of the seriousness of the client. It also gets you some money at the point when the client feels most urgently about the project. Once you have solved the problem, it comes to seem less urgent to the client, who may take his time paying you.

A good invoice has the word "INVOICE" in large, bold letters. Workers in the accounts payable department do not deal in nuance. You must make it clear that this is an official demand to be paid. Obviously, it should also include the date very prominently. The invoice is what sets the payment clock ticking.

When I send an invoice, I make reference to the contract or purchase order. If it is a purchase order, it has a unique number to which you must refer on your bill. You may also have a vendor number that you should include.

You shouldn't be wordy about the products or services delivered; such matters are specified in the contract or purchase order. But you should say something brief and clear, so that those processing your bill will have something to refer to if there is a problem. Expenses that have been authorized should be clearly marked and listed separately. (And don't forget to include taxes and surcharges you have paid.)

Most importantly, the invoice should say how much is due you, and when. If you want immediate payment, you should say "Payment on receipt of invoice." Otherwise you should state your terms, such as "Net seven days," or "Net 30 days." You may find it advantageous to offer a discount for immediate payment. If so, state it clearly on your invoice.

Always make sure that your invoice is clear and businesslike. It's a minor detail, perhaps, but your livelihood depends on it.

Getting paid

Everybody likes to get paid. But hardly anybody likes to ask for payment.

Too often, once you finish your work, that's only the beginning of the struggle. This is a shocking realization for those who become spare room tycoons after years of being handed a regular paycheck. But it is nevertheless part of life. You can minimize the problem by dealing with the issue before you begin, not after you finish. Even so, I sometimes find myself, for one reason or another, making exceptions that have come back to haunt me.

One such case started with my feeling rather ebullient. *Your Company*, a magazine published by American Express and Time Inc. for owners of small businesses, had written an article about how I had helped one of my clients move into Asia. It ran my picture. I sounded like a miracle worker. If you can't believe your own publicity, at least for a few hours, why bother at all?

The day the magazine came out, I got a call from a vice-president of a local manufacturing company. He told me the article struck a chord because he had been frustrated trying to sell to China, and he had ceased to trust the agent he was using. He asked me how much I would charge to schedule a short management briefing on selling equipment in China. I quoted a number that was far less than I normally charge. The company headquarters was only 15 minutes from my house, and it is my experience that companies are more likely to hire a consultant who is nearby. Besides, the subject was one I know well, so there was little need to prepare. I also failed to demand at least partial payment in advance. I figured it was more valuable to me to get in the door.

After our conversation, I expected authorization for the job to come in a few days, and when it didn't arrive in a few weeks, I forgot about it. Then the telephone rang a few months later, and the vice-president told me he wanted to go ahead. By this time, I had second thoughts about the low fee, but I had made a promise, so I went ahead. The presentation was very successful. The company's owner, his son the vice-president, the controller and other key managers attended. They took me out to lunch, and we discussed my working for them in the future. It was a good day.

The following day, I sent an invoice for the presentation. A month went by without payment. I began to feel uncomfortable. I faxed a copy of the invoice to the company. No response. I mailed a copy of the invoice to the vice-president. Silence. I began to be angry at them for ignoring me, and at myself for waiving my policy of prepayment. I called the accounting department. The person who answered my call told me that someone would get back to me "at their own convenience." What an insult. I was not a beggar. I had done my job and done it well.

Sixty days after the talk, with no check in the mail, I was becoming both enraged and insecure. I felt that the company had decided simply not to pay me, just because I am small. Their letter of invitation was a valid contract, but perhaps they figured that the amount was too small to justify the expense of a lawsuit. This was a sum I could clearly live without, but it became an obsession merely because I interpreted their failure to pay as a conscious act of disrespect.

Finally, nearly three months after the talk, I reached the vice-president on the phone. He seemed surprised that I hadn't been paid, and he had the controller, who seemed to have particularly enjoyed my talk, get back to me. He asked for the amount and date of my invoice, and two days later, I had the check.

I still don't know what happened. It seems to have been such a small sum that it just fell through the cracks of the company's payment system. It wasn't an act of hostility toward me.

And part of the fault was mine. If I had kept to my usual policies, I would have been paid in a timely manner and never have wasted so much energy. By asking for so little, with nothing in advance, I may have devalued my services, and made myself into something too small to worry about.

But this incident reaffirmed my conviction that one of the chief jobs of the self-employed is to see that we get paid, if not quickly, at least eventually. It's easy to see this as dirty work, somehow beneath our dignity. But there's no need to be shy. Don't sit around, conjuring up paranoid scenarios. Clients forget sometimes. They must put out so many fires that paying you isn't a top priority. Sometimes you have to become one of those fires, and— as pleasantly as you can—make a nuisance of yourself. You have to create a situation where paying you is the easiest way out.

Don't expect gratitude from customers

Spare room tycoons need good customers and good clients. These are people and organizations who have the need, the budget, an understanding that what you offer is needed. They also respect you and treat you well. You say this is a very stringent definition. You bet. Good customers and clients are hard to find.

Most customers happen to have a need. And you happen to be around. When they need you, and they have the budget to buy what you offer, they can be very charming. But once the goods are delivered or the job is done, and they don't need you any more, they will more than likely forget you.

Don't get me wrong. We need those who use the products or services we offer. And we should give them respect and the benefit of the doubt. But it is foolhardy for self-employed people to expect a pat on the shoulder, a thank-you card in the mail, or a letter of appreciation written without request. On rare occasions, clients do that. There are some very nice people around. But the majority are just consumers. They, like us, have their own fears, insecurities, anxieties, and crises to cope with at work or at home. Frankly, they simply can't think about you too. You should be happy that you get paid on time, or get paid at all.

Some try to low-ball you. Others simply want to pick your brain without paying you for your experience and expertise. Some mistrust you because they fear that you might steal their jobs.

Your responsibility is to do a professional job in every case. You shouldn't be resentful of the work you

put in to get the job done. It may have been more difficult—and more crucial—than the customer realizes.
That's life.

Do your job, and let go. Be cordial and respectful, but
keep a distance. You don't need to get chummy. And
when you get no gratitude, you feel no resentment.

It can be frustrating if nobody tells you whether you
have succeeded in your tasks. When there is no one to
affirm that you're good, it is hard to believe that you are.
Unlike in schools and colleges, there are no grades, no
certificates, no diplomas, no measuring of how good you
are when you complete a job. There aren't even employee
evaluations. The only measures are the level of the bank
account—an important though not always entirely accu-
rate indicator—and our own assessments. Such self-
evaluations can be brutal. Often, I have been
unrealistically tough in judging myself. I'm a pretty hard
boss to work for.

One indication of your usefulness is if clients keep
using you over and over again. But sometimes, things
change and they no longer need you. They'll say good-
bye, your job is done. And like the lone gunman of the
Wild West, you will move on, knowing that you've saved
the lives of those who've sought your help, too wise to
expect any thanks.

❖❖❖

There are few things more difficult than placing a value
on what you offer. Nevertheless, money is the reality
principle of business. When customers won't pay what
you need to charge, that can mean only one thing: you're

in the wrong business. And if you try to charge less than you need to survive, that will also put you out of business. You'll simply be working harder as you fail.

Sustaining

8
Balancing Work and Life

Most of us become spare room tycoons for reasons of our own. We are trying to integrate our lives and our livelihoods in a way that fits us better than the ready-made careers offered in the employment market.

Some of us, for example, are looking for ways to spend more time with our families, even if we're working during much of the time we're doing so. Others seek to make their work embody their values, fulfill a personal myth, or express unique talents. Still others want to live in a particular place or in a particular way, and create their own businesses to support these aspirations.

These are aspirations that can be fulfilled. Parents, for example, are returning to their households in force, without giving up their second source of income. Houses are increasingly becoming places where goods and services are produced, not simply places on which money is spent. Even though much of this activity is made possible by the computer—that icon of modernity—we are, in some respects, returning to the premodern home in which work and family life were carried on incessantly, inseparably, and by every member of the household.

We may, however, underestimate how radical a change this is. Most of us have been accustomed to a clear distinction between work and family life. We feel that we have the right to reward ourselves for our labors, often by making our private lives and our leisure activities more elaborate. When there is no clear demarcation, work intrudes on private life at the most inopportune moments. Conversely, if we're not careful, the obligations we feel to family and friends can decimate our productive time.

Moreover, the very technology that makes it possible for many of us to work on our own—email, cell phones, fax machines—tends to make everything in our business lives more urgent. Our clients and customers are increasingly able to find us any time and anywhere, and they expect an instantaneous response. Even employees complain nowadays that they are never off the job. But for spare room tycoons, the problem is even more acute.

The very advantages of the lives we have chosen can often present some of the most pressing problems. It is good to be with one's children, but often their needs conflict with what has to be done. Many of us like the convenience and cost savings of working from our homes, but we must guard against the business taking over all our home life. In an ideal world, our businesses would all have rooms of their own with doors that can be closed when we leave to live the rest of our lives. More often, though, work invades personal space like a particularly aggressive fast-growing weed. We must be vigilant, or else we will be hopelessly entangled.

Finding the proper balance between work life and private life is something with which all independent business persons must grapple. Some believe in drawing a clear line between the two, but that's easier said than done. Not many of us can simply ignore a ringing telephone. It could be the next big opportunity. It could be a family emergency. We answer the phone and are often derailed from what we planned to be doing. To be able to ignore a ringing telephone, is, I have concluded, the beginning of sanity.

Many are looking for something even more elusive, an integration of work life with personal desires. This requires being clear about what we expect from our work and our life. Both need, in some way, to be compromised in order to reach the optimum result. It can be tough to find exactly the right mix.

Friends and family members raise other issues. Often they don't realize how different our lives are from theirs. Because they view houses as places of leisure, they confuse working at home with not working. They may also see the flexibility we seek as spare room tycoons as an indication that what we do isn't serious. When, for example, there is an emergency involving an aging parent, the self-employed sibling is often able to be first on the scene. But your employed brothers and sisters might also expect you to see the crisis through to the end. After all, they have jobs to return to, and they believe you don't.

At times, it seems impossible to find a balance between work and private life. Bear in mind, though, that this is probably why you went into business for yourself in the first place.

Another nutty entrepreneur

I'll admit that I'm not a great role model for balancing work and leisure. I try to prevent my business from completely swallowing up my personal life, but often I fail. One important reason for this is my upbringing, which prepared me well to be a spare room tycoon, but less well for having a life of my own.

I grew up not knowing that there should be a separation between life and work. My mother ran a dry-goods store. We opened our store at 9 am and closed it at 10 pm, daily, all year round. We were never closed except maybe once each year on New Year's Day. We ate lunch and dinner at the store. Customers would still come in while we ate; and we would interrupt meal times to sell.

There were many moments, especially in adolescence, when I wished we had a family life. I longed for moments when I could have my parents' undivided attention. I wished we were in a home where people could not walk in off the street.

My situation was, in fact, the way most children have grown up in most times and places around the world. The family was, first and foremost, dedicated to economic survival. Children work from the time they can walk. Leisure is a rare exception, not a daily expectation.

I think there are some good things about such a life. Although I did not have many private moments with my parents, I was with them all the time, not separated from them as are so many children of contemporary households where both parents work. I held a sense of responsibility toward the family, and I grew up feeling that I could handle myself well with other people. I think that we spare room tycoons have an opportunity to set a good example for our own children about what work really entails, and that we should encourage them to help us out, when it's appropriate.

Comparing what I lived through as a teenager to what I have been doing over the last 17 years as a consultant working in a home office, I have a great deal of privacy. My business has a space of its own, and I can shut the door and sleep peacefully without hearing and worrying about the urgent faxes that come in during the night. I serve only a handful of customers at a time. People don't walk into my home office from the street. I have a great deal of autonomy.

Yet I still have not completely escaped from the lifelong experience as a teenager growing up in a store. It took me many years to tell myself that it is worthwhile to have time that is reserved for one's life.

In the beginning of my practice, I was so intent on making my venture a success that work was the only reason to exist. Whenever I felt tired or depressed, I would give myself pep talks and I became easily self-motivated. I was rarely immobilized for more than a day.

Over the years, I have come to realize that working all the time may take its toll on me. The problem of continually working shows up in the feeling that nothing is really meaningful. Even making money is not fun any more. And when unpleasant things happen, they become even more irritating. The final indication of burnout is a loss of interest in everything.

There is no reason to work oneself to death. On those occasions when I feel that I'm turning into another nutty entrepreneur, I attempt to walk out on my own job.

I go to the museum, take a long, aimless walk in the city, read a novel, or sit in a park and just stare at the buildings, the sunlight, and the people around me.

We need time to lie fallow, to get rid of the waste of daily emotions that wear us down until we lose interest in anything. To me, nothing is worse than feeling that there is no meaning in what I do. When I catch myself feeling that way, I know that I should break away.

Heartburn

Rocky Condino was 25 when he started his heating and air conditioning business in 1979, and he was determined to succeed.

He was doing just about every job in the business—salesman, installer, repairman, bookkeeper. And he never stopped.

His day began at 7 am, and most nights it would be about 11 pm before he got back home. He barely had time to say hello to his wife. He was oblivious to their two babies.

And even once he was home, he kept on working. As he lay in bed, he was thinking about what he needed to do the next day, and what steps he should take to make his business grow. "I was five steps ahead of myself all the time," Rocky recalls.

The business did grow, partly because of Rocky's diligence and enterprise, and partly because he had started it just as a real estate boom was getting under way in his market area. People were building new buildings and investing in old ones. Some felt prosperous and treated themselves to central air conditioning for the first time.

Throughout the 1980s, sales increased at least 10 percent each year, and as much as 20 percent in a few of the best years. Because Rocky now had a dozen or more employees, he was now taking personnel problems to bed with him. He worried about how he could get his workers to perform up to his standards, and to stop arguing with one another.

In addition to working 16 hours a day during the week, he also put in 12 hours on Saturday and 4 on Sunday, his easy day. "I regret now," he says, "that I didn't see my kids grow up in their early years." When his wife speaks, for example, of when the babies started to walk, he draws a blank. He wasn't there.

Although he felt stress, he says, "The work always came." The business was growing in a way that fulfilled his expectations. He had nine trucks. His employees wore spotless uniforms and gloves, and were trained always to wipe their feet before they entered customers' homes.

Anticipating more growth, he rented a 10,000 square foot showroom and spent $50,000 just on the expenses of moving in. He had a new logo designed, and he bought television advertising during hockey games. He was delighted when friends and neighbors commented on the ads. He had an aura of success.

At night, though, it was a different story. His sleep was troubled by acid reflux, which his doctor told him was caused, in large part, by anxiety. Several times he awoke in panic, fearing that he might choke to death. "Don't let the business kill you," his doctor told him.

"Just because you have money, it doesn't mean you don't have stress," Rocky observes. "Growth has real costs."

Suddenly, the growth stopped. In the early 1990s, sales started to decline even faster than they had been rising, even as Rocky had higher overhead costs than ever before. Believing that he had an exceptional group of employees who would be difficult to replace, he decided to keep them on. But after a year of declining business, he had to let them go. "What took me ten years of good times to accumulate, it took me two years of recession to spend," Rocky says.

Reluctantly, he decided to move out of the fancy showroom into the small building on a dead-end alley where he had started his business.

He was still in business, but he was back to the beginning. Finally, he resolved to do things differently. He decided to have a life. He decided to make more time for his personal life, and to establish a strict separation, so that neither his work nor personal life is allowed to interfere with the other.

"When I pull into my driveway at the end of the work day, the business is the farthest thing from my mind," Rocky says. He compares what he has done to installing a switch in his mind. When he gets home, he turns the business switch off. He allows no shop talk. Even when he socializes with one of his employees, he never discusses work.

Rocky still works hard, but he makes sure to have dinner at home at least four nights a week. "When you sit down and eat dinner with your family, everything comes up," he says. "You talk about their day. Family becomes closer."

Rocky had long been a heavy smoker, but at his family's urging, he cut that out. He joined a health club, and took up racketball. When he has a tough day, he will work out his frustrations on the court rather than stew in them all night.

Rocky often works on Saturday, but he nevertheless designates it as a calm day. He will, for example, go to the shop by himself and clean it up, then go home to mow the lawn and take care of his vegetable garden. On Saturday night he takes the family out to dinner.

Occasionally, he violates his policy of not over-working, but he says he pays attention when his wife asks what's bothering him. That question is her signal that she thinks he's pushing too hard.

Rocky made it through the recession, and during the good times of the late 1990s, word of mouth gave him all the business he needed. He has expanded a little, but he learned not to try so hard to prove himself a success.

Nobody will ever call Rocky laid back. Indeed, you could argue that he has pursued having a personal life as zealously as he once threw himself into his business. But he is not sick any more.

Raising a family while you work

One of the paradoxes of being in business on your own is that you are more aware than most employees that you rely on others to survive. It's difficult to achieve independence without having some people in your family, your community, and your profession on whom you can depend.

Such people become an informal support mechanism: They listen to our complaints, keep us from becoming too self-absorbed, and help us with routine chores when a deadline looms. Such people are lifesavers, but they can sometimes become problems too.

Margie Brogan, a labor arbitrator, knows this more than most. Her profession is about resolving conflicts between competing interests. Likewise, different aspects of her career and personal life are frequently in conflict, and she can't deal with them like the calm, blindfolded figure of justice with her scales. Finding a balance often means she has to scramble.

Being an arbitrator is typically an old man's profession, the sort of thing some people do part-time in retirement after they have spent a lifetime making contacts. Margie is a mother with three children who works at the job full-time. When I talked with her, she was booked up 10 months in advance. She is doing very well after some lean years when assignments were scarce.

Margie, a lawyer, was on the staff of the National Labor Relations Board for six years. She liked the work, but when she had her first child, she cut back to three days a week to spend more time with her. When she had a son a couple of years later, she quit the job altogether, intending to freelance and to teach labor law part-time at a nearby university. In 1990, she set herself up in business as an independent labor arbitrator.

During that time, she saw herself as a mother first, which was a good thing because cases were far and few between. It's the nature of the job that it will take lawyers, judges and union leaders a few years to become aware that you are available. Fortunately, her husband had a good job with sufficient income to support the family.

While Margie had sought a job that would give her the flexibility to be a good mother to her children, she

still wanted to have a profession. Some of her most difficult moments came on those occasions when she did get
work. Fortunately, she lived in a very close-knit neighborhood in the Philadelphia suburb of Narberth. She had
frequently watched her neighbors' children when their
parents had an emergency, and, when she began to be
busy, she called in a few of these favors and sent her children to stay with the neighbors.

Margie believes that had she lived in a less friendly
or caring neighborhood, she would have had a more difficult time making her business work. She says her business wouldn't support the cost of full-time daycare for her
three children, and even if it did, that's not what she
wanted. "I could not have raised a family and built a business outside of the community," she says. "Friends and
the community have made it all possible."

Margie seems to be striking a good balance, overall,
but she is the first to acknowledge that, as her business
has grown, there have been tensions between her mater-
nal and professional roles. When her youngest child was
born six years ago, she stayed up late the night before his
birth writing a decision, then dropped it off on the way
to the hospital. Once, when her business was just starting
to take off, she was called by a reporter for a major newspaper as her children screamed in the background. She
asked the reporter to call back in five minutes, turned on
the television, filled the coffee table with junk food, and
took the telephone into the closet.

She is quick to point out that the noise wouldn't
have distracted her. "I can work with two TVs on," she
boasts. "I've learned to work anyplace, anytime with any
amount of noise."

Nevertheless, she recently moved into an office of her own, not far from her house, largely to keep her distance from some of the people who have been so helpful to her as her business developed.

"When you work out of a house, people don't view you as working," she says. "One time, I was in the midst of a conference call with two lawyers, and a friend walked into the house and started talking to me as if I weren't doing anything at all. Now, when I go to my office, friends realize that I am really working."

Pictures of sanity

When I was first in touch with Thys van der Merwe, a self-employed computer programmer based in Richards Bay, on the northeast coast of South Africa, he mentioned offhandedly that he had a website. "It's probably not of much interest to your work," he said. "It is focused on my biggest hobby which is photography—my way of staying sane in the self-employment environment."

Needless to say, I was very interested: I'm always on the lookout for ways to stay sane. And once I called up the site (http://home.mweb.co.za/te/teknovis), I became more interested still. These pictures of the wildlife and landscapes of South Africa are hardly weekend snapshots. They reflect a serious commitment, an artistic sensibility and, one suspects, heroic patience in waiting for the perfect shot.

"To me," says Thys, "photography, like computer programming, is an art form that is bound by certain rules. It is different enough to help me escape the stresses of self-employment by moving my mind to a different level of creativity, but it still has enough touch with reality for me to be aware of the constraints of technology and the medium I am using. It puts your mind on a level not present in a work environment."

When he decides to make a photograph, Thys says, he feels as if the world takes on the quality of a dream that he wants to recreate in the picture. "Whether it works in the end as a 'winning shot' is irrelevant," he says. "It has helped me, for a short time, to look at the world in a different way and see things I would normally have passed by."

He finds this different vision not only when he is out in the bush taking the photographs, but also when he gets home and processes and selects them.

"I'm going through a very tough patch right now, with a deadline looming and software bugs making life difficult," Thys reports. "I have about 60 rolls of film still lying unframed in a box. For the last two weeks, I have spent at least an hour before I go to bed examining and framing slides. When I am under pressure, it is like a little escape to look forward to every day. It calms me down and relaxes my mind completely."

Thys has always been dedicated to outdoor sports, as a competitive hang glider, rock climber and scuba diver. He says he decided to drop those risky activities and concentrate on photography in 1994, once he opted to take on the responsibilities of self-employment. But, he adds, the outdoor, physical quality of nature photography is an important part of what engrosses him, and it provides a strong contrast to the abstract, sedentary task of computer programming.

Moreover, during a time when many other highly trained white South Africans have been leaving the country, Thys has felt a desire to immerse himself in the landscape of his native land. His photographs have encouraged him to do so. "The photography is more about getting into the bush," he says, "than it is about snapping the shutter."

Photography played a role in his recent move from the bustling Johannesburg–Pretoria region, where he was able to get many high-paid assignments, to Richards Bay, where jobs are fewer and the pay not quite as high, but which is closer to the places where he enjoys taking photographs.

"I think that regularly taking on more work than can be handled in a normal working day is one of the pitfalls of self-employment," Thys says. He took a few days off in Richards Bay to decide whether he could handle some high-stress assignments he was being offered, and that's when he heard of the possibility of getting work there.

His wife Ester, with whom he takes the photographs, approved of the move, and she became a spare room tycoon as well, running a paging and communications equipment company that she and Thys bought. Thus the photography, in addition to providing him with an artistic and emotional outlet, also induced the couple to change where and how they live.

Thys is not, then, making a strict separation between his avocation as a photographer and his paying work as a programmer. Both of these are part of his life, and his desire to do photography has helped shape his recent career moves.

He has even found that his photography has helped him to establish better relations with his business clients. "When they notice my photographs," he says, "many people want to see more, and I do that by holding very informal and relaxing slide shows. I find it very important to be able to reach my clients on a personal level outside the work environment. This has worked wonderfully for me."

Walk in the woods

One of the benefits of being a spare room tycoon is that the commute is short. For me, it's just a single flight of stairs. I know others who live and work in the same room, and still others who, as their business and staff have expanded, have created offices in the basement, the garage, and the garden shed as they have tried to keep home and business together.

But this desire to keep the business within your personal domain creates the danger that you might become insular and lose the all-important sense of balance. Every waking moment seems to be part of your business. You worry over leaving the house for fear that the phone will ring and you will miss out on great opportunities.

Yet, there is great value in leaving the house, even if you have nowhere to go. It gives you a chance to stand apart from your business, perhaps even to think about something else.

I know one spare room tycoon who has staff members in every nook and cranny of his suburban house. And every morning he leaves the house and drives somewhere. He thinks about his life. He thinks about what he should have done yesterday or what problems he didn't solve. Then he drives home, and arrives at the "office" at the same time as his employees.

Helen Solomons, a former corporate executive who founded her own human resources firm, Harrison Associates, in 1986, believes that one of the best things about independence is that it allows you to follow your own style of work. "I was 'on stage' all the time when I was a corporate executive," she says. "I hated it. I wore clothes that didn't feel right to me. People worshipped my position, but I had no idea of whether they respected me."

Her most recent venture, a computer software system that helps companies to manage telecommuters, is a logical outgrowth of her interest in allowing people to work productively in their own ways. It has been extremely successful. "I've succeeded in everything I've set out to do," she says.

Part of the freedom she feels now that she is her own boss is that she can wake up in the morning, see that it's a beautiful day, and give herself some time off. "In a company, the boss often feels that if he can't see you at your office, you must be goofing off," she says. "They don't understand that employees learn to mentally leave their job by staring at the computer and a spreadsheet."

It's better, though, to escape into fresh air and sunshine. Helen lives near a large park, criss-crossed with hiking trails, and she frequently leaves her home office to take a five-mile walk. She believes the time is highly productive. She thinks about what she has been doing, and how to be better at what she does. She doesn't go out on the trail with an agenda; one of the benefits of getting out of familiar settings and moving around is that you jolt your thinking and get out of intellectual ruts.

"Very often," she says, "I come back from a walk in the woods with the solution to a problem that had been a terrible puzzle."

A modern hermit

When I tried to get in touch with Jan Opdyke, it took me a while to reach her because she was camping out in the Michigan woods, hunting for morels. Jan's business is to prepare scholarly writing for publication. In her year, the morel season comes right after the dissertation season.

A great deal has been written in the last several years about how information and communications technologies decentralize things. People speak of the electronic cottage, a place where you can be away from it all, while still at the center of things. Most electronic cottages I've heard of tend to be second houses clinging to the side of a mountain, from which a vacationing CEO can hurl an après-ski thunderbolt.

Jan lives in a log cabin in Michigan, but her spirit is more Walden Pond than Aspen. She finds it odd that she would show up in a book called *Spare Room Tycoon*, for several reasons. For one thing, her cabin is a single room. More importantly, her work, which she enjoys, supports a low-income, low-consumption lifestyle. She has no interest in expanding her business. Her goal is to "be in nature" and achieve peace of mind. "I am happy, but poor," she says.

Yet I think she belongs in the book because she is actually living out a fantasy that many independent people entertain, at least from time to time. She has truly escaped the rat race and taken up a way of life that has rhythms very different from workaday existence.

Jan discovered her country retreat when she was working at the University of Michigan, in Ann Arbor. Recently divorced, she bought the remote cabin, which cost less than her car, so that she would have a place to get away from academic life, which she found rewarding but stressful. The three-hour drive to get to and from the cabin eventually proved stressful in itself. She would drive out on Friday night, and it would take her till Sunday afternoon to really relax, then it would be time to drive back to Ann Arbor. When her Jeep's odometer turned 100,000 miles, she decided to live differently.

In her job at the University of Michigan, she had established enough contacts at university presses and other scholarly publishers to feel confident that she could get enough assignments to live a simple life in the woods without starving or freezing to death.

"I live in the kind of place where people go for a couple of weeks a year and indulge in dreams of packing it in and moving to the country," she says. "The reality is very different. Unlike being on vacation, the usual cares and responsibilities of life follow you here. Second, oohing and aahing over the landscape quickly gives way to the practicalities of dealing with it. There is much more physical labor involved with living here than living with the conveniences of the city."

Jan was surprised to find that she missed some aspects of the life she had left behind that she had scarcely considered before. One was the cachet of her old job and the distinguished people with whom she had worked. "I must have invested more in that prestige than

I had thought, but I found myself throwing my previous position in the faces of people here who couldn't care less," she says.

She's over that now, she feels. Because she is a single woman living in a log cabin in the woods, "some people think I'm kind of weird, a character. I guess that goes with the territory. I'm a hermit at heart. I crave the contemplative life."

The other difficult adjustment—even though it's part of the reason she moved to the woods—was accepting how powerfully the environment sets her agenda there. "If you want to go to town on Tuesday and there's a snowstorm, you go Wednesday or Thursday," she says. "If you want to stay warm this winter, you get your firewood up now. Railing against it does no good. I find that when I begin to get frustrated or unhappy, it's because I'm trying to control something uncontrollable. It took me a good two years to recognize this."

Such a life is something few people can sustain. I know that I would get restless after a few hours. Like friends who visit her in the cabin, I'd begin to want to go to the movies or check out a mall.

For Jan, being on her own in this way holds enormous satisfactions. "Perhaps there are fewer distractions standing in the way of a direct confrontation with the infinite, questions of life and death and meaning," she speculates. "Perhaps one is more receptive. Here such questions seem to stare you in the face every day. I would happily grapple with them for the rest of my life."

Home office, personal space

Just about the last place I would expect to find serenity is in the financial markets. Every second promises a new crisis, a new opportunity. For some people, the constant and instant change is an addiction, more compelling than life itself.

Nevertheless, of all the people I interviewed for this book, Rochana and Richard Norby, who own a financial planning firm, probably come closest to being at peace with both their business and their life. They work very hard, but they maintain an absolute separation between their work and their business. What's even more important, they don't seem to worry about missing business opportunities while they are living their lives.

Their business, advising wealthy people on how to invest their money, is inherently less nerve-wracking than Richard's previous career at an options-trading firm. They try to cultivate a measure of serenity in their clients as well, encouraging them to think, as Rochana says, "about what money can do and what it cannot do."

Rochana and Richard literally put work and life in their proper places, and they allocate specific times for their business and private lives as well. They live with their two children and work in a large suburban house. The ground floor consists of a main office where they meet with clients, and two other offices, occupied by a secretary and a sales assistant. The upper floor is their home, a very private space.

Every Sunday evening, Rochana and Richard have a meeting to plan their schedule for the coming week, and post the schedule on the refrigerator door. The schedule says who is going to prepare lunch and dinner on each day. It says who will take their son to his piano lesson, for example, and delineates every other family responsibility that they can anticipate. "We want to do a lot of things," Rochana says. "The week becomes very chaotic if we don't plan."

Like many spare room tycoons, the Norbys work in the evening. But they do not work on Tuesday or Friday or weekend evenings. These are solely for family and personal activities.

The two rise each morning and exercise in Valley Forge National Park, which is adjacent to their home office. Afterwards, they come home and have breakfast together. They also have dinner with their children every night. "We consider meal times sacred," she says.

There are no telephones on the residential floor of their house. Once they go up the stairs, they are out of reach of clients, relatives and friends. Anyone who wants to reach them must do so during their business hours. They do have a cell phone for emergencies. But they have trained themselves not to jump to answer the phone.

"In order to take care of other people," Richard says, "we have to take care of our mental health."

They also take substantial time off, both around Christmas and in the summer. Richard likes to use some of his time off to do volunteer work, such as preparing food for homeless people. They also use the time to meditate and practice their religion.

"When I'm away, I'm really away," Richard says. He believes that the more they give in their charitable work, the more they gain in return, both spiritually and materially. "Sometimes we are flooded with work when we come back from volunteering," he adds.

During their time off, the two say that they don't give any thought to promoting their business, or even worrying about it. "We don't have to promote ourselves," Richard says, "we get as much business as we can handle."

Paradoxical as it seems, their conviction that money isn't everything may actually help them to attract and retain clients. They cultivate long-term relationships. "Each of our clients is a friend," says Rochana. She noted that they don't keep a computer in the office where they meet clients, because they want their clients to feel that they are paying full attention to them. "Without a computer, the room has a welcoming feeling to clients," Rochana says. They often serve tea, or sometimes lunch.

Such an approach is not for everyone, but Richard and Rochana don't want everyone, just enough clients so that they can support themselves and live a balanced life. Rochana grants that nobody can predict when large clients will leave or when new ones will appear. She says she tries to be prepared for life's ups and downs—which is, after all, the very thing they are helping their clients to do as well.

She avoids vague dread by quantifying what can go wrong, and seeing that she is protected. "If you want to drive 80 miles an hour, and you know that if you are caught, you will have to pay $80, then put the $80 in the glove compartment," she explains. "When you are caught, you just give up the $80."

"Our priority is to have a steady mind," said Richard. "We want to be content, to be centered, to have a goal in life and not just go rushing through life."

"The goal is not to have to work 24 hours a day," added Richard. "You must know whether you see work as your life—or whether it is the part of your life that supports the rest."

❖❖❖

Becoming a spare room tycoon is, for many, a search for wholeness. Integrating a good career into a good life is a worthwhile and attainable goal. But it can also be a difficult challenge. There will inevitably be conflicts, and you should expect to devote energy and creativity to resolving, or at least managing, them.

It's a paradox that finding integrity often means creating boundaries. If you have enough space to work with, providing a physical separation for your business is the easiest way to start. Not everyone has this luxury, though, and some don't feel they need it. Nevertheless, just about everyone should give some real thought to how they allocate their time, and make sure that the business doesn't crowd out everything else.

The proper balance between work life and personal life is something that changes over time. It can change, for example, with the ages of your children, or with the evolution of your own goals and interests. When you first start your business, it will demand all your time, and most of the effort you put into it will be justifiable. But even at that crucial moment, you should still make sure that you make room for other things. Otherwise you may form self-destructive habits that are hard to break.

Each of us responds to the challenges of creating an integrated life individually. The accommodations we make reflect the sort of people we want to be. What's important to remember, though, is that balance does not just magically appear. We all have to work at it.

9
Daily Anxiety

Everyone feels anxieties, and we spare room tycoons have many reasons to feel anxious. When business and profits are coming in, we worry whether they will continue. When the world seems to have forgotten that we exist, we fret over whether we're in the right business, or even whether we will survive.

Some of us may be able to suppress such anxieties, or ignore them. Most, though, will always have them. The real issue is not how to make the anxieties go away but rather how to at least keep them from being destructive and ideally put them to good use.

I think it's possible to use the daily anxieties of self-employment the way actors use stage fright, as a way of sharpening and giving urgency to the way they perform. Indeed, many people seem to use their careers as a means of overcoming their anxieties. For example, a shy person who is afraid to use the telephone becomes a journalist and needs to call people continually. The computer whiz who likes to work out technological puzzles by himself goes into business fixing other people's computers, knowing that everyone will be looking over his shoulder. Such anxieties never go away, but necessity keeps them under control.

Anxiety is most acute at those moments when you don't know what to do next. You can help tame it by establishing routines. A bonus is that, in the name of banishing your fear, you can also accomplish necessary tasks that you don't much feel like doing. When left undone, such uninspiring chores can themselves be a source of anxiety.

Anxieties come when we are alone in silence. The solution is to talk to other people. This can be not merely calming but very informative.

Our workplaces can be hives of anxiety. It's important to get out regularly so that we don't feel trapped in what we are doing. Go for a walk. Take a vacation. When you do, you elude your anxieties, at least temporarily, and return with answers to questions you didn't even know you had.

Sane self-deployment

I've known Jim, an insurance executive, for more than 20 years, and I've always considered him, in some ways, to be the opposite of me. He's a perfect employee, well briefed, good at what he does, adept at dealing with external pressures, and able to deflect the fallout of messy situations away from himself. Lately, though, he has been showing subtle signs of curiosity about going out on his own, so he was very interested when he heard I was going to write a book about it.

"You've got to do a chapter," he said, "on what you do when you get up in the morning."

If he hadn't said this, the idea never would have occurred to me. I'm rarely at a loss about what to do in the morning. Many days, there's a pileup of work that needs to be attended to. When it's eight in the morning at my office in Philadelphia, it's eight—or sometimes nine—at night in Shanghai and Beijing. Some people have a hard time getting started on their work, but I don't have that luxury. The very brief period during which I can reach people in Asia virtually forces me to swallow some coffee, then hit the ground running.

While I have been sleeping, Asia has been generating crises, problems that can be exasperating but nonetheless form the basis of my livelihood. A heap of paper in the inbox of my fax machine often begins to tell the tale, though this must be followed up with telephone calls both to agents and business contacts in China and my clients in North America to sort out the problems. Then I write memos, both for my clients and my own records, to help me keep track of where matters stand. Often, by the time I have things under control, the morning is gone.

I think that Jim, who often functions as a trouble-shooter within the big company for which he works, would recognize what I do in the morning, even though he can't understand all the languages I do it in.

But I realize, too, that this is not really the question he is asking. He is wondering about moving from a life where he takes the same train to his office each morning, arrives at the same time, and operates within an organization with well-defined rules, procedures, and expectations, to one he defines himself. He is wondering about those first mornings, when you don't have the clients who do the business that generate the crises and the faxes. He is wondering about replacing the external discipline of the corporate world with an order of his own making. Corporate life often has too much structure, too many silly rules, yet at least some of them have to be replaced when you go into business for yourself.

I seem to have an easier time of this than many. I know several self-employed people who are extremely efficient when they have a project to finish, but who go to pieces when the pressure for immediate performance subsides. And when you're self-employed, one of the things that will make you fall apart is uncertainty about where your next dollar is coming from. I've always believed that getting new jobs is one of my most important jobs. Thus, on mornings when there's no grief coming from the other side of the globe and my projects here are under control, I work on direct mail, faxing and other ways to promote my business.

That doesn't mean that you shouldn't take advantage of the flexibility of working for yourself. There are some mornings when the most productive thing you can do is take a walk and let stray thoughts come into your mind. One morning, I realized that the next few days wouldn't be busy, then I noticed a newspaper advertisement for cheap, last-minute airfares. Two mornings later, I was in Utah, hiking in Zion National Park, savoring the freedom of being a spare room tycoon.

But these moments of freedom must come within a disciplined structure. Otherwise, you don't have the money to pay the airfare.

Make the phone ring

The great fear of the spare room tycoon is to be forgotten. It's bad enough when people know about you, but don't need you. It's worse to feel that nobody is thinking about you at all. You feel like a gadget left neglected in the back of the drawer, still useful, but utterly forgotten. You just want to scream "Get me out of here!"

For me, the most powerful trigger for this particular terror is a silent telephone. There are days when I'm extremely busy, juggling the work of three or four clients with scarcely a moment to spare, and telephone calls are likely to be a distraction, if not a nuisance. But even on such busy, money-making days, I feel I need a little action from the outside world. If the phone doesn't ring, at least there could be a fax. Where is the UPS lady? The Fedex guy? "Sorry, you have no email messages." How dare you! Doesn't anyone on earth care about me? Then the phone rings, and it's someone who wants to talk about my long-distance calling plan. That interruption only makes the silence more unbearable.

Nevertheless silence, and often a deadly feeling of loneliness, are the frequent companions of the self-employed. It can be just as insidious in good times as bad because a silent office seems to portend lean times ahead. The spare room tycoon is never home free.

The phone that rings regularly seems to be an indicator of well-being, akin to a proper pulse rate or a healthy complexion. The phone needs to ring to keep my spirits up, but how do you make it happen?

As a longtime user of direct mail and faxing campaigns, I know that even when I drag sacks full of letters to the post box, there's no guarantee that the telephone will ring. Besides, the first one to call is likely to be a competitor trying to check you out, or a middle manager who responds merely in an attempt to look busy to his superiors. These are troublesome calls that I'm happy to do without. Yet even such insidious or exasperating calls often feel better than silence.

It took me close to a decade to discover something that ought to be obvious. The people who will make your telephone ring are people you already know. For me, they can be people I've met at professional gatherings. They can be people who have attended my seminars, with whom I've established a rapport. They can be former clients who have moved into other jobs where they don't need my services, but still are happy to talk about their own situations. They can be personal friends I haven't seen in a while.

I used to be reluctant to call such people without an agenda, but I've discovered that "We haven't talked in a while, and I want to stay in touch" works for most people. (Obviously, you can't use it on the same person too often.) Such people nearly always return my calls, and that means that when the telephone rings, there's often someone at the other end I'd like to hear from.

Not too surprisingly, these calls sometimes turn out to be useful. On a couple of admittedly rare occasions they have brought me new work. More often, those I've called have been willing to share information that has proven useful to me. But it's unrealistic to think that making such calls will "pay off" in any immediate and quantifiable way.

What they offer is something that the spare room tycoon sorely needs, a sense of perspective. They let me get a take on the world from someone else's point of view. They offer a taste of the workplace sociability that is often what those of us who work independently miss most. Having the benefit of others' perspectives has a long-term business benefit. It helps me craft promotions to which others might respond. Explaining yourself to someone sympathetic is good practice for making a pitch to someone skeptical. And hearing what others are talking about gives insight into the culture as a whole, which is an antidote to letting the business absorb all our attention.

But I never look to an immediate profit from staying in touch with lots of people. The reassurance of having the telephone jingle on a day when the office feels like a mausoleum is payoff enough.

The plumber and the dentist

For most people who offer services or products, other people's anxieties are the source of our business. People are willing to pay us because we can solve their problems. But not all problems are equally urgent. One of the most common anxieties of spare room tycoons is whether people really need what we offer.

Not long after I started out, my kitchen sink sprung a serious leak and I called a plumber. I was grateful when he arrived. I didn't ask him what he was going to do. He finished his job and presented me with a bill that I didn't question. I paid him on the spot.

I was, momentarily, delighted that my house was no longer filling with water. Then I began to be depressed because, while the plumber must wade into crises regularly, his business seems free of the worries and insecurities that haunt me daily.

I reflected that even when potential clients call me, we generally have lengthy conversations in which they express skepticism about what I can really do for them. Then, typically, I submit a proposal that details exactly what I intend to do and includes the amount I plan to charge, a figure that usually involves some agonizing calculation. Then, sometimes, the client might have questions about the proposal and add or subtract responsibilities. Getting the go-ahead to start work can sometimes take months. And a client who pays the moment that the services are performed is a rare and wonderful thing. If, like my plumber, I stood and waited for my check, my client would probably have me committed to an insane asylum.

Most self-employed people have reason to be jealous of their plumbers. That's because the needs to which we minister are not so urgent as a flooded kitchen or a backed-up toilet. Yet we are problem solvers too, and we soon learn that the messier the situation you are called on to deal with, the easier it is to make the sale, and the faster you can collect your payment.

I sometimes feel sympathy for my clients because doing business in Asia can be difficult, and they run into problems they never expected. I can't afford to feel too bad, however, because if there were no problems at all, and everything always went smoothly, they'd never have any need for my services. Like the plumber, I depend for my livelihood on the certainty that things will go wrong. At the same time, I probably couldn't survive if things became so difficult, and so many things went wrong, that my potential clients became discouraged and simply gave up.

Nobody will use you, and pay the fees you have to charge, unless they believe their problems are urgent—and you can solve them.

Not long ago, my dentist convinced me to have him perform a long-delayed and very expensive procedure. Because I had felt no pain, I didn't have any sense of urgency about it. Still, because I remembered excruciating agony from past dental problems, I eventually gave in.

I was behaving like my clients. Most of them have had unpleasant experiences they don't want to repeat. So slowly, reluctantly, deliberately, they decide to use me because they remember the pain.

Under control

Bill Wollheim is a sort of plumber for the information age. He fixes problems that are less dramatic than a burst pipe but equally catastrophic: computers that have died or gone berserk.

Bill operates a one-man business out of his apartment on Roosevelt Island, in the middle of New York's East River. He has been doing what he does for 18 years. He now has a client list of nearly 300 small businesses and individuals who can feel secure that if things go awry, Bill himself will be right over. In other words, he's a spare room tycoon who makes a good living from serving others much like himself. "I'm the person they feel is responsible for their computer system," he says.

Bill feels that he has been assuaging, or causing, technological anxiety all his life. One of his earliest memories

was setting up an AM radio, an FM radio and the television for an early experiment in stereo broadcasting, and
sending his Aunt Ida into a panic. She was afraid that by
turning on so many things at once, he would burn the
house down.

Bill's education is in English literature. His business
grew from a hobby, and a conviction that he didn't want
to let technology pass him by. He bought his first computer in 1982. Since then, the personal computer has
grown from a cultists' toy to a necessity of life. Bill has
opted not to grow with it; he has chosen to remain a one-
person business. "I want to build a business, but not an
empire," he says. "If I build the business too big, all I'll be
is a manager."

It turns out that even Bill envies the plumber and the
dentist, because the people whose problems they treat
rarely try to second guess them. "People feel that they
ought to know about computers," he says, and he believes
that although most of his customers like him, they feel it's
a failure to have to call him. They stand over him and
watch closely, in the hope that they'll learn enough not to
have to call him again.

Bill's problem is that computers are so complex that
he often has to go down several blind alleys before he
finds a way to solve the problem. "If you're lucky, the
clients think you're a genius, and if you're unlucky, they
think you're a moron." Bill says he tends to be a rather shy
person. The feeling that he is always on stage is, he says,
very stressful. He can't help feeling nervous when his
work is watched so closely, but he is, at least, used to it.
"So many things are out of control, and the client wants
me to be in control," he says.

Besides, whatever stress he feels now is insignificant compared with the way he felt when he worked for others. "I spent years in therapy trying to figure out why I was not happy working for people," he says. "I finally quit seeing a therapist and started building my business. Now, I have the luxury of feeling fulfilled."

The illusion of security

As we have already seen, spare room tycoons are always looking for a breakthrough—that big job that will establish the business and keep income rolling in for a good long time. But, as Steve Sherretta learned, what seems to be a breakthrough can turn into an ordeal.

The breakthrough came at a time when Steve really needed it. His corporate communications business was experiencing some lean times. He was doing one of the most difficult things for most spare room tycoons: making cold calls to prospective clients. He tried calling a company that he thought would be a dream client, an $8 billion healthcare company. Discouraged, he had a vision of this company, and others like it, employing an army of secretaries and receptionists to fend off people like himself. The point is to fight your way through to someone who might be at least slightly receptive.

So Steve was shocked when the first person he reached actually seemed to be glad that he had called. She told him that she thought a particular person would be the right person to talk with, and she put the call through immediately.

Steve was delighted but suspicious. "I thought to myself that this potential client must be absolutely desperate," he says. "She had to have a deadline looming, or someone leaving, or something going on." His suspicions were aroused further when the woman who later became his client actually got on the telephone. She didn't want to see samples of his work. She didn't want to meet him face to face in order to see whether they could work together. What she mostly wanted to know was how much he would charge and how quickly he could start work on a corporate brochure. She hired him during this initial conversation.

Steve had been in business for five years, and this just didn't feel right. "It had never happened before," he says, "and it has never happened since." In some ways, though, it felt good. Steve needed the work. The client didn't quibble with the fees Steve quoted. The client was big and well-known—a great addition to his portfolio. Nobody can afford to look a gift breakthrough in the mouth.

Still, even this good news produced anxieties. After the client had agreed to his fees and he had started work, she asked for samples of his work to show to her superiors. Steve thought a well-organized executive would have asked for the samples and had the internal politics in place before making a commitment. "I just felt there was something queer about this procedure," he says.

He went ahead and did the brochure. She told him she loved it. The brochure was printed and Steve was paid. Steve learned that his client was empowered to make important decisions, so he pitched her a more ambitious ongoing job—a newsletter that could be circulated to 20,000 pharmacies throughout the US.

She thought it was a great idea. She met Steve for lunch and told him to prepare a slide presentation to sell his idea. He did so, and he waited for a response. And he waited some more. Then he sent emails that went unanswered, and made calls that were never returned. "I was getting angry," Steve said. "She is a flake. Her behavior is unprofessional."

Finally, after weeks of this, he reached her on the phone, and she spoke as if there had been no delay in returning the call. She was enthusiastic about the newsletter, she said. And she invited him to lunch again. She wanted to add a writer familiar with pharmacy retailing, and a graphic designer whose work Steve didn't admire.

The four-page annual newsletter he had proposed was metamorphosing into a 36-page glossy magazine to be published several times a year. Steve began to see visions of major new revenues and an expanded business. The team went to work on the first issue, and once that was brought to its final stage of production before printing, began work on the second. Things were moving so fast on this project that Steve turned down another, well-paying project from an older, smaller client so that he could focus on this high-profile assignment.

Then, just as the first issue was about to go to press, things took a turn for the worse. The huge company was about to be absorbed by an even larger one. Because there were antitrust issues, everything was thrown into limbo. As in all mergers, employees were understandably fearful that they would lose their jobs, and were afraid to commit to decisions. But due to the possibility that the government would stop the merger, this period of uncertainty dragged on and on. Finally, the merger was canceled, and the president of the company even commissioned Steve to write the letter that went out over the president's signature to customers and shareholders explaining what had taken place.

Even when the crisis was resolved, the first issue of the new magazine was delayed month after month. Steve had slowed his work on the second issue, and finally after about four months of uncertainty, word came from the client to stop work. Then she dropped out of sight again, failing to return calls or emails. Steve learned, through the rumor mill, that she was going through an extremely ugly divorce. During the trial, her husband threatened in open court to kill her. "I have great sympathy for the woman," he says. "She was going through hell."

He still felt that she ought to have returned his calls. It wouldn't have been difficult for her to tell him that the projects had simply been canceled. But it preyed on Steve's mind that she was simply showing him no respect whatsoever. He later found that an out-of-state advertising agency was getting the business she had once given him.

This wasn't really a disaster for Steve. He was paid for nearly all the work he did. He added a prestigious name to his client list. It would have been better if he hadn't turned down other work, but his injury was less financial than emotional. He was hoping so much that the break-through was real. He allowed his mental state to be dictated by the obviously erratic behavior of the client. His relationship with the client began in anxiety and ended in insult. But only in retrospect can one see that the casual way in which the client hired Steve mirrors the cavalier way in which she cast him aside.

What, then, should Steve have done? Nobody would argue that his niggling insecurities at the outset should have told him to forgo the opportunity. Perhaps his mistake was to make this assignment too important in his own mind. "I fell into the trap of thinking that the project would become self-funding and safe," he says. There are few things that cause more anxiety than the aspiration to safety; suddenly everything life throws at you jeopardizes your illusion of security.

"There is nothing I could have done," says Steve. "It all had nothing to do with the quality of my work. It had nothing to do with me." Nevertheless, he did learn that the magic, effortless good fortune we all hope for can often bring even more abundant and intense anxieties than does the daily grind of trying to stay in business.

Six worries

Nine years after leaving her job as a lawyer for the US Postal Service and setting up her law practice as a sole practitioner, Mariann Schick has come to know her anxieties very well. There are six principal ones, she says, and they torment her regularly. Unlike the Muses of mythology who inspire, these unwelcome visitors get in the way, though she has learned to work despite them.

The first of them, she says, is the cashflow anxiety. When she set up her practice, Mariann thought she would be able to build the amount she bills in a linear fashion from month to month and year to year, but she has found, instead, that while expenses must be paid regularly, income follows cycles.

Some of these are predictable. "Nobody gets a divorce in the summer," she says, and as a consequence, that part of her income goes down. "Nobody does any business over Christmas," she adds, and then her income virtually disappears.

The unpredictable cycles are even more terrifying. "Two years in a row," she explains, "business slowed down in May and didn't pick up until November. Clients may come in all at once, and there are whole periods of time when no one calls."

The second anxiety is meeting payroll. "I hate to owe money," she says. And because both her father and mother were deeply committed to the labor movement, she feels strongly that she must treat people who work for her fairly. Besides, good secretaries need to be paid well, or they will go elsewhere. "When I have hired bad secretaries, I feel like I'm working for them," she says. Sometimes, cashflow isn't strong enough for her to afford office help, and she lets them go. But she will never allow herself to be late paying them.

The third anxiety is being a one-person firm. Mariann must return her clients' calls herself. Often, she can't delay talking to a client until she is ready. "Clients want to be able to reach you," she says. "They'll remember if they can't." Besides, many clients might prefer to work with a firm that offers many services and specialties. She worries whether there is any future for a sole practitioner lawyer.

The fourth anxiety is being a single woman. "I'm not a lonely person, but I am a single professional woman," she says. "There is no one to take care of me but me." She sometimes fantasizes about living in a time when women could stay at home with the family and depend on men to support the household financially. "This idea that women should take care of themselves has been much overblown," she says, laughing to signal that she really doesn't mean it. But the worry is real.

The fifth anxiety is billing. Many of her clients are employees of the federal government or Postal Service, people who may have been discriminated against or wrongfully terminated. They don't have a lot of money, and to them Mariann's hourly rate of $275 seems extremely high. Other firms charge more, she says, but "$275 is a lot of money."

During the first few years of her practice, she tried charging lower rates for clients whom she felt would have difficulty paying. But she found that she was not making enough money to sustain her practice. "I feel cold-blooded," she says when she tells them she cannot represent them because they can't afford her rates. "It is just a reality of life. I still have to pay my Visa bill."

The sixth anxiety is about making the business grow. She would like to be able to practice law full time, rather than spending much of her energy running the business, serving as a therapist for clients, promoting her services, lecturing and doing all the things that large firms hire support staffs to do. She thinks about trying to expand, but the first five anxieties have tended to hold her back.

"The anxieties of working for myself get to me," she says. "I don't want to do this for another 15 years."

But she can imagine one thing that would be worse. "I hope I'm never in the position where I have to go back and work for somebody else," she says. "I'd rather have these anxieties than the depression and angst of working for somebody else."

❖❖❖

Anxieties are the constant companions of the spare room tycoon. Properly used, they can help us fight complacency and force us to get to work. But when they are bad enough, or allowed to loom too large, they can get in the way. They fester when we are isolated, and attack when we don't know what to do.

I have found that anxieties are less troublesome when I'm busy. A regular routine helps keep them at bay. So does keeping in touch with people. Making the phone ring combats the terrors of silence and isolation. So does getting out of the office, so that you can exercise and perhaps jog your thinking in unexpected and productive ways.

It's worth remembering that what we sell to or do for others is a result of their anxieties. Most of us would be out of business if everyone stopped worrying. What we can't do, though, is let our customers' fears, worries and irrational behavior threaten our precarious stability. Our own anxieties are troubling enough. We can't afford to take on others' terrors as well.

10
Good Times, Bad Times

Spare room tycoons want control over their lives. This is why we want to start and run our own businesses. Yet we know that we are really never in control either over people or the course of events. What we get is the illusion of control, much as employees who get their weekly pay checks get the illusion of security.

Sooner or later, everyone who goes into business is going to suffer reversals. Sometimes these are wakeup calls that teach us something useful. But they can also threaten the very survival of our enterprise. The possibility, and thus the fear, of failure is something we must live with, but we shouldn't let it debilitate us. There are far worse things that can happen. Besides, people live through failure, and spring back all the time.

This is why we must learn to rejoice when times are good. We need to admit, and remind ourselves from time to time, that we have succeeded in what we do—simply because we have been able to keep doing it and make a living at it.

Some people seem to have more difficulty coping with good times and reveling in their success than they do when they are facing adversity. To admit that things are going pretty well seems to be tempting fate. That's something you shouldn't worry about, because something bad is probably going to happen eventually, whether you enjoyed the good times or not. The key is to survive the setbacks, and you have a better chance of doing so if you get your energy from joy rather than from fear.

That is, I know, a lot easier said than done. It is perversely tempting to search the clear blue sky for dark, ominous clouds. These storms will come, but we must learn to enjoy the sunshine.

Once you've experienced some ups and downs in your business, you realize that it is pointless to fear future setbacks. You mustn't lose sight of the fact that the realization of our independence is reason for celebration.

This willingness to accept success, to feel that there is a reason to be joyful, despite the knowledge that bad times will come, is an enormous asset—a gift that we spare room tycoons can give to ourselves.

The joy of survival

Today I walked into the bank where I opened my first account when I started my business. That was 1983. I had very little money, though the bank was happy to take all I had.

I had a dream I was convinced would work. Worrying comes naturally to me, so of course I had some trepidation, but I also felt the thrill of making a bold move that was going to change and improve my life.

When I needed some money to get the business going, though, I found that the bank did not share my enthusiasm. The reason was simple. I didn't have a job. I was a bad risk. Only by getting someone who was employed to vouch for me could I get any money at all.

At the time, the bank was Philadelphia National Bank. A few years later, my business was a little bigger, the bank was called CoreStates, and none of the people I dealt with before were still working there. Now the bank is called First Union, and there's a whole new cast of characters. I have to call North Carolina to get anything accomplished.

I'm not happy that the people who turned me down for a loan have lost their jobs. They were only following the institution's standards. But their situation does remind me that the supposed stability of full-time employment is often an illusion. I'm still only a one-man operation, but I'm still here and making a living at what I like to do.

I think of one of my first clients, a corporate executive I had always seen, and depended on, to have an extraordinarily stable work situation. He worked for an impetuous, eccentric, somewhat arbitrary man, a former spare room tycoon who had invented an extremely successful product. "Every day as I was driving to work," my client told me later, "I had the idea in the back of my mind that today was the day I would either be fired or quit." This went on for 17 years, and then one day he was right.

In the years I have been in business for myself, I have had many fears and have learned to live with them. I don't ever want to feel that my career depends on another person's whim. Maybe that's what makes my client such a good employee, while I'm destined to be independent.

As I walked home from the bank, I had a feeling, not of elation exactly, but of really deep satisfaction. I don't own a Rolex, unless you count the one I bought from a street vendor in Bangkok. I've never felt I needed a Mercedes. But success can happen in less showy, less expensive ways. I have helped people. I have enjoyed myself. There is no need to live in fear, or lurch from crisis to crisis.

The point is to keep your head up, to follow your heart, to ride out the highs and lows. While the bank saw me as an accident waiting to happen, I saw myself as an individual about to be realized. And I was right.

Strategic retreat

"Once you've seen a ghost," goes a Chinese saying, "you'll always be afraid of the dark."

Count me among the frightened, then, because I've come face to face with the specter that self-employed people want least to encounter: business failure.

I got through this dark patch by making what I now see as a strategic retreat. But it seemed like failure at the time.

For the first four years I had my business, income was increasing year after year. I was able to afford vacations, a new car, and even a house that actually had a spare room I could use as my office. There was stress, but I was extremely confident overall.

The fifth year, gross income declined for the first time, but only a little. The next year, it declined some more. The euphoria over China had ended, as was inevitable, though I still was being asked for proposals. Fewer and fewer were being accepted, however. The following year, I had to start using some of my savings to pay my fixed expenses. Then the ghost appeared.

In June 1989, the Chinese army fired on students in Tiananmen Square in Beijing who were protesting corruption, nepotism and lack of freedom. The whole world saw the students' idealism and the government's violence. Will anyone forget the picture of a lone man, trying to stand up to a tank?

A few months before, a very large company had asked me to submit a proposal to help them establish several new operations in China. It promised to be the breakthrough for which I had been hoping. They spent a lot of time mulling over the proposal, and I was growing very impatient. But the smoke had hardly cleared in Tiananmen Square before they gave me an answer. In view of the chaos in that country, they said, this was not a time to enter.

Before long, other clients were calling and telling me that they wouldn't need me—at least until things sorted themselves out. I couldn't really blame them. During that period of uncertainty, I wasn't sure I wanted to go to China myself.

Only then did I start to face the real likelihood that my business was in trouble. I didn't want to go back to a nine-to-five corporate job. But there was really little choice. I didn't want to deplete my savings, and prospects for more consulting business were bleak. I started to look for work.

I did direct mail, answered ads, talked to friends. At one job interview, the employer contemptuously walked out in the middle and went to the bathroom for half an hour. I felt he was telling me that, even though I was used to being my own boss, if I worked for him I would have to show my subservience every day.

One afternoon, my telephone rang. It was the president of a company that was about an hour's drive from my house. He needed someone to handle unruly Asian suppliers, including the manager of the company's Taiwan office. He wanted me to start right away. The salary was quite attractive.

When I showed up on a sleety January day in 1990, I found that not all the company's problems were in Taiwan. Its founder had agreed to sell the business to the man who hired me, but he was having second thoughts. He was hiring and firing executives left and right. (Six months later, he even fired his chosen successor, the man who hired me.) My new employer was nearly as despotic and unstable as China. My two hours of commuting were the only part of the day I enjoyed.

Fortunately, when I took the job, I asked two of my ongoing clients if they wanted me to continue to work for them on nights and weekends. I wasn't willing to let my business disappear entirely. And it worked well for my clients. They didn't want to do much in China right then, but neither did they want to give up. I found the work I did for them much more satisfying than for my employer.

Finally, after 16 months on the job and seeing 11 top executives come and go, it was time for me to leave as well. It was as if a storm had lifted. I was able to expand the work I did for my two ongoing clients, and new ones came along. I have had healthy growth each year since— though I know the ghost is out there.

And one very odd thing has happened. I frequently find myself making use of knowledge I acquired during the time I felt I was in exile. If I had fretted less about how taking the job had certified me as a failure, I probably would have learned far more.

When you're on your own, it often seems that every reversal of fortune is your own fault. But sometimes, things happen that you are powerless to resist. I was caught in a geopolitical storm. There was no choice but to retreat and wait for it to blow over.

Finding refuge when disaster strikes doesn't make you a failure. It's great to succeed. It's essential to survive.

Surviving success

Gary Samartino hasn't just seen the ghost. He knows it personally.

The technical documentation business that he started with a partner did well enough in the first three years for them to hire an employee. Then business dried up, and they kept the business going for far too long. It failed, leaving only debts behind.

Gary is sole owner of Infoventions, which he founded in 1993. In many ways, the history of the firm is similar to that of his previous venture. He had a couple of years of very good business, then there was a falloff in workload. Gary took a course in sales and marketing, but despite his efforts, nothing was happening. He was still paying bills from the previous business. Gary hung on, but barely. He worried about supporting his three children.

Finally, after several years of this, Gary's wife gave him an order: "Get a job!" He hated the thought, though he understood the necessity.

Just as he was about to admit defeat and start his job search, the phone rang. It was a former customer who was working for a new company, and needed some help. This turned out to be a very large project, one demanding and lucrative enough to allow him to postpone his job search.

Then another customer for whom he had been doing small jobs came up with a larger one, then some new clients came in. In short order, Gary had more work than he could handle. Remembering his recent drought, he didn't dare turn anything down. He hired some subcontractors to help him.

At this point, a very large job that he had pitched for nearly two years before came through. This sounds like a truly happy ending. But when you are in business for yourself, there really is no happily ever after. Particularly, if you have stared failure in the face, you cannot afford to coast on your success.

Gary is still running from the ghost. He doesn't dare turn anything down. Before he knew it, he had 10 people working for him on various projects. He has become a manager, without quite meaning to, though he insists on doing much of the work himself and checking closely on the rest.

He often works until two or three in the morning. He sometimes sleeps at his office. He is able to have dinner with his family only about once a week. He worries that he has little family life. When he does go home, he feels that his daughter has become distant. "She doesn't want to feel rejected if she becomes too intimate with me, and I'm not there," he says, recalling his own childhood when his salesman father was often absent. "I know how it was when Dad wasn't home."

He says his wife is pleased that his business has turned around and there is more income in the household, but she is very unhappy that it means that he has disappeared. "We don't have a relationship any more!" she told him recently.

Gary believes that if work keeps up as it has, he will be able to retire in a few years. But by then, it might be too late for him to be a good father to his children or a good husband to his wife.

Gary's problem isn't that he is greedy. Rather, it is that he views his current success as a very short-term condition. If he felt confident that his business would continue at its current volume, he would give it a more permanent structure, one that would allow it to run if Gary weren't there 16 hours a day, seven days a week. He would be able to take a long weekend, perhaps even a vacation. He has the money for it. Instead, he conceives of what is, in effect, an 11-person firm as a one-man operation with 10 stopgap helpers.

Gary is riding a tiger; he dares not dismount. I can certainly sympathize with his feeling. Every independent business person has experienced the feasts, and especially the famines.

Yet it's also important to create a business that can survive success as well as failure. If you've encountered the ghost, you'll never forget it. But you must try not to let yourself be haunted by it.

A business plan for hard times

One way to calm your worries about bad times is to structure your business so that it is more likely to survive a downturn. That's what Carol Aitken has done.

Carol and her former husband, a scientist who studied moon rocks, moved to Houston with their five-month-old daughter just in time to catch the 1970s oil boom. Carol didn't know exactly what she wanted to do, but the area was so prosperous she was certain that, when she was ready to go back to work she would find something.

One day she answered an ad in a Houston newspaper that an employment agency had placed for a local manufacturer. She didn't get that job, but soon she got an offer from the employment agency itself. Despite a total lack of experience, she got a job as a personnel recruiter. She did well at it, and rose to the number two position in the firm. More than 50 recruiters reported to her. She was pulling in a generous salary, and enjoyed all the executive perks. But she wasn't really satisfied to be even so important a number two. She wanted to be in charge. In 1979, she left the firm and started her own.

She didn't take any clients with her. One of her former assistants asked to come with her, and she agreed. On the first day in her new office, she found herself with a phone, a legal pad, a pen, and an employee. She was a divorced mother of two with no alimony and no income. She recalls: "I sat there thinking 'Oh, God, what have I done?'"

Fortunately, she knew her business, she knew how to write effective advertisements, and the economic wind was still at her back. She found good candidates. She found good jobs. Pretty soon she was doing good business.

One day in January 1980, Carol received an assignment that disturbed her. An oil company executive wanted her to prepare for the outplacement of 20 executives. This was the first time she had been asked to do this. "Recruiters know before most people when bad things are about to happen," Carol says. She figured that she had better batten down for difficult times.

She immediately began to shrink her own office by placing her employees in new jobs. She moved to a smaller office. She started focusing her marketing on Houston-based companies that did much of their business elsewhere. She leased her big house with a swimming pool, and moved into a smaller town house. The rental fee provided a small income, and she could still borrow against the value of the house, if necessary.

By April, the end of the oil boom was announced on the front pages of the newspapers. The *Yellow Pages* directory shrank that year from five inches thick to an inch and a half. Home foreclosures became commonplace events. The number of employment recruitment companies in the region shrank from 1100 to 100.

"I know how to compete in a down market," Carol says. "I'm convinced that eight years make a cycle." She believes that for any business to have staying power, you have to be ready for the down times, and not be afraid to take immediate action to cope with them.

Family problems drew her to the Northeast, so she sold her Houston business and took a job in Baltimore. Once again, she was unhappy as an employee, and after a year she was running her own employment agency once again. She wasn't working in a boom town, as she had in Houston, but she benefited from the general good times of the 1980s.

Then in 1990, around the time Saddam Hussein's army invaded Kuwait, Carol saw some danger signs once again. Facing the second down market of her business life, Carol was determined not to be dependent on the regional economy. She looked for a recession-proof niche. She decided to focus on the IBM AS400 computer.

As Carol saw it, while this machine was not the sexiest technology around, it was the bedrock on which worldwide information and communications systems were being built. It was a machine that was generating jobs for programmers, chief information officers and many other sorts of workers.

She began to cultivate relationships with programmers. She joined their society, attended their conferences and volunteered to help organize their activities. She befriended the engineer who developed the AS400. She became a well-known person in this narrow but important field. People will answer her calls and ignore those of other recruiters. And her pool of jobs and talent is worldwide.

Her business has not become as big as it did in Houston, and she has no aspirations for it to do so. "I've done my empire building," she says. "My ego has been fulfilled." What she has now, she believes, is a small business that has a good chance of surviving.

Life after catastrophe

In 1990, Robert J. Booker felt like he was on top of the world. He owned a company that was the sole supplier of a key component of IBM's mainframes. Another product was part of the US Army's bombs. He also made assemblies for General Electric and other large companies. His product line of spare parts was diverse and not dependent on any single industry.

He also felt that he was benefiting his fellow African Americans. His inner-city factory was running three shifts around the clock, and most of the workers were highly skilled black workers whose previous employers had departed for suburban locations. He was considered a leader of the community and was proud to think of himself as a role model who might inspire other African American young people to educate themselves and contribute to the community.

"I really thought that life at that point was just a question of bringing in more orders, retiring my debts and then just growing," Robert says.

His first worry came during the summer of 1991 when IBM sent a team of engineers to review the quality and capability of the factory. "They were rude and abrasive, and I thought they were looking for reasons to terminate us as a contractor," he explains. But at the end of a full day of poking around the plant and asking pointed questions, the head of the team told Robert that the visit was occasioned by IBM's desire to increase its order. "He told me that they had to find out if we were as good as they thought we were, and that we had passed the test." The order was increased by 30 percent.

Then, only three weeks after the big new order had come through, IBM told Robert that the company would cancel all its orders. The mainframe business had essentially collapsed, and IBM was left with an enormous and expensive inventory. Robert's business with IBM was over.

Three months after that, Robert got word from the Army that it was canceling all of its orders for military spare parts. The end of the Cold War was forcing cancellation of weapons orders and spurring the consolidation of defense contractors. This was a second, damaging blow.

Less dramatically, but just as devastating to Robert's business, was the emergence of China as a major supplier of industrial components. With their low labor costs, the Chinese could make electronic cable assemblies for less than 10 percent of Robert's costs. The diversity of products and customers in which he had placed his faith did Robert no good. China's cost advantage was so compelling that nearly all his customers disappeared.

"I had worked hard during all of my career," Robert says. "I worked long hours. I didn't do drugs or girls. I didn't have a pretentious lifestyle. Then my world collapsed all around me."

He says it pained him to lay off his employees. In many cases, both husband and wife worked at the plant to support their families. He knew that the loss of their jobs would devastate his workers, because in that place and time there were literally no other opportunities. But Robert had little choice. Soon, the business was bankrupt.

Still, he was an entrepreneur, and he retained faith in his basic approach. The success of his previous business was, he felt, his ability to identify a highly skilled labor force that nobody else had recognized, mostly because few had cars to commute to jobs outside of the city.

"Opportunity exists where there is either a problem or there is no competition," Robert says. He recalls a football coach who used to tell him, "Take this ball and run it where they ain't."

He spent a lot of time trying to analyze what he should do next, though his current career began more or less by accident. Some friends had asked him to help out with a newspaper they were thinking of starting. Robert was interested in newspapers because he has strong convictions about how African Americans should deal with racism and poverty.

"Black people look at government, the law, and politics as the way to remedy the evils of racism, repression and injustice," he says. "Since these types of remediation have never worked anywhere, any time in the history of the world, the faith of black people in these institutions has always seemed misplaced to me. The link between the white world and the black world is money."

So Robert started looking at the economic power of African Americans in the Philadelphia region. He found that the black and Hispanic population living in the city's suburban ring earned $11 billion each year, but that there was no advertising medium directed specifically at them.

"Just about every other ethnic or community group has its own newspaper," he says. "Jewish Americans, Italian Americans, even debutantes have their own newspaper. It is well known that African Americans are huge consumers. We save less and spend more than other ethnic groups."

In 1996, Robert started the *Suburban Black Journal*, a monthly circulated to 80,000 readers. He is the sole proprietor and half of a staff of two. He hires freelance writers, some of whom have views with which he strongly disagrees. "The goal is to stimulate my readers' interest," he says. "My sole purpose is to make money."

Robert is working out of his house. He is no longer a powerful industrialist. But he is back in business, looking once again to find an opportunity in the African American community that others ignored.

From cancer to career

In November 1997, Christina Pirello became a star. That's when her program *Christina Cooks* began to be broadcast on public television stations throughout the US. Hers was the first cooking program to make a macrobiotic diet— devoid of meats and heavy on grains and vegetables— palatable to a mainstream television audience. Overnight, she went from teaching a few people at a time how to cook her way to addressing a national audience. This was an exciting moment, a vindication of what she believes in.

She wouldn't be having these good times, however, if she had not had a terribly bad time. At the age of 26, she was diagnosed with leukemia. Her doctor told her that she had only six months to live. Christina's mother had died of cancer, so she had some idea of what lay ahead. In any case, she decided to quit her job at an advertising agency and spend the short time she thought she still had doing things she liked.

While she was telling this story to her employer, a fellow employee was eavesdropping. He told Christina that he was acquainted with a man who knew how to recover from cancer by changing one's diet. Christina wasn't particularly hopeful, but she figured that she had little to lose. The man was Robert Pirello, who told her that he had gotten the idea from a book written by a Japanese thinker, Michio Kushi.

Christina followed the diet, and within 18 months, she had a complete remission of her leukemia. She also married Robert Pirello. "My doctor told me, 'Sometimes God just makes a miracle,'" Christina recalls. "He also said, 'Food will not make you better.'"

Christina, though, was inclined to place her faith in the diet. In any event, she says, it makes people feel better. Having grown up as a butcher's daughter, disgusted by the blood and guts endemic to her father's work, she was so grateful to get her life back that she became an evangelist for whole grains and vegetables.

In 1987, she began teaching cooking classes out of her home, charging each student $25 for a three-hour cooking lesson. She then compiled her recipes into a cookbook, and started to try to get on television.

Because she cared more about getting her message out than about making money right away, she accepted an arrangement with a local PBS station to do the show without any payment, other than an announcement of a number to call to order her cookbook at the end of each half-hour program.

She is very grateful for the widespread acceptance of the program, but success brought costs she didn't anticipate. "We were selling books like crazy," she says. But she quickly found herself paying high legal fees to protect her image and her recipes. The producer was taking a cut of her book sales, and the stations that ran it were taking another cut. She found that she was overpaying for the toll-free number for taking orders.

Indeed, her overnight success brought about so many new expenses that her husband, Robert, who had been working with Christina in her business, had to take a job to pay the bills.

In the long term, of course, the exposure is giving Christina some exciting new opportunities. Robert has returned to working with her and finding underwriters for the show, and making sure it continues to be aired and is promoted. Christina has been told that she has the potential to become "the Martha Stewart of macrobiotic cooking."

Christina and Robert are still the only employees of their business, which remains in their home. But even Michio Kushi, the guru who started it all, told her recently, "If you don't move out of your home, you cannot grow."

Christina respects the advice of the man whose ideas she credits with saving her life. But she adds, "My goal is never to build an empire. I want to tell people how they can have their health."

❖❖❖

Good things happen all the time, and too often we take them for granted. Terrible things also happen. They're part of life. The only issue is whether we are going to interpret them as evidence of failure, or merely as temporary setbacks.

The knowledge that days won't always be sunny can have constructive consequences. Bad times offer good lessons to help you weather even more severe storms ahead. Nevertheless, fixating on the possibility that things will take a turn for the worse can prevent us from noticing the good times while they're happening.

11

How Big Do You Need to Be?

Should you remain a one-person business? Could you offer better services more profitably if you were larger? These are issues that just about everyone who starts a business faces, and because business conditions change over time, they never really go away.

You can't make a plant grow by pulling on it. So says an ancient Chinese proverb, one that I think applies to us spare room tycoons. In most cases, our businesses need to be well-rooted—with steady customers, a track record, expanding prospects and sufficient capital reserves—before we should even think about growing.

There are obviously some exceptions. In internet businesses during the last few years, the basic idea seems to have been the most valuable, and vulnerable, part of a business. People with good ideas need to rush to make their businesses attractive enough to support an initial public offering, or to be sold to a larger company.

But most spare room tycoons aren't involved in this sort of mania. We need to be assured that our businesses have sustainable natural growth before we take on the additional overhead and labor costs that come with expansion. We have seen in earlier chapters how rapid expansion can add to the stress you feel, and how the normal ups and downs of business can make an overextended business fail.

It is important, too, for you to consider whether you are expanding because your business justifies it and you find it fulfilling, or whether by becoming bigger you are merely trying to prove that you are successful. Think twice before you buy into the cliché that bigger is better. Creating a larger firm will most likely require you to spend more of your time managing others than doing what you set out to do.

Moreover, you might find yourself growing into a company that is large enough to be slow and bureaucratic, but not large enough to be a strong player. There is much to be said for being small and agile, and for sticking to the area where your talents lie. If your core talent and passion is managing, your goal should be to expand. All the rest of us should think twice.

Obviously, this book has a bias toward those who have decided to stay small, because if they have grown larger they are no longer spare room tycoons. We like the flexibility of being able to create and recreate our own businesses. Many of us have employees and many more take on staff and independent contractors to help us deal with particular projects. This has become known as the "virtual" company, though I think its great virtue is that it is a versatile company, one poised to take advantage of a wide range of opportunities.

We spare room tycoons are at the cutting edge. Our small size gives us the freedom to be creative and experimental. Perhaps the Intels, Daimler-Chryslers and Time-Warners of the world have a similar freedom, but not the smallish and middle-sized firms we would likely become if we were to expand.

While I was researching the book, I met a young woman whom I sought to interview. She works in a creative support capacity in the film, television and advertising industries. She has some important ongoing clients, including a long-running television program. She is the only full-time member of her company, but she employs a stable of more than a dozen people on a project basis. But she didn't want to be in the book because she doesn't consider that she has a business. She just believes that she is working as an individual, trying to get by. If she had a business, she told me, then she could sell it and make some money from it. She would like to have a business some day, she said, but couldn't claim to have one now.

I don't know what her plans might be, but I think an attitude like hers can be dangerous. She is apparently prosperous, she does extremely interesting things, she appears overall to be happy, but she seems somehow convinced that what she is doing isn't a real business. If you feel that way, you might easily be tempted to expand the business in conventional and counterproductive directions. The business might appear more corporate and "serious," but the expansion could divert your energies from the things you do well toward other chores at which you are, at best, mediocre.

Not everything that grows on the earth is destined to be an oak tree. Besides, most plants would be grotesque if they could grow as large. And they can't because they don't have the proper structure; gravity would bring them down.

What's important isn't simply to grow but to flourish. And many of us—more all the time—have learned to flourish while staying small.

Soloist or string quartet?

When I first set up my business, I concentrated on promoting my services to the largest corporations that were involved in the most ambitious, best-publicized business operations in Asia. What I'd often find was that these companies had in-house managers who were jealous of their turf and not likely to use a consultant, or that they used huge, multinational consulting firms whose bureaucratic structures mirror those of the large corporations for which they work.

Thus, I thought that I had scored a breakthrough when an important manager of a large pharmaceutical corporation called me in for an interview. He told me that the firm was thinking of becoming active in the China market, but wasn't sure how to begin. We talked for about 90 minutes, long enough for me to conclude that he was interested in what I had to offer. He concluded the meeting by asking for a proposal. This was a very encouraging sign.

I agonized over the proposal—especially the fee, of course. Then I sent it in and heard nothing for several weeks. I then called to follow up. The executive with whom I had spoken was very amiable, and he thanked me for spending time and writing the proposal. Then he told me, essentially, that I had been wasting my time from the very beginning.

"We are a large, multinational company," he said. "If

we were to hire a consultant, we would have to find a large consulting company. We couldn't even consider a one-man firm." I told him that I thought I could assemble a team of people with the specialties necessary to serve his account more effectively and efficiently than the consulting behemoths. "Then all you would be is a string quartet," he said. "We wouldn't handle a string quartet."

He said this without rancor, without any note of criticism, as if it were simply the way of the world. And, in a sense, it is. "Nobody gets fired for buying IBM," as the saying used to go. You hire a consultant for brand name advice. Mine might have been better, but I was nobody.

A short time later, the company was swallowed up by an even larger international firm. Presumably they would now need the combined forces of the Vienna Philharmonic, La Scala and the Mormon Tabernacle Choir to produce a nugget of wisdom that such a behemoth could digest.

"He was stupid," said a friend to whom I recently told this story. "The Rolling Stones are a sort of string quartet, but they've been filling arenas for decades. And the Three Tenors are, let's face it, only three tenors. What you have to do is amplify yourself, present yourself as someone who's so special you deserve to be listened to."

My friend is right, in at least one respect. My proposal, and perhaps especially my fees, were too modest to be taken seriously. But while I may actually be the Mick Jagger of China trade consultants, I have not yet been accepted by the corporate world as a superstar.

I have, however, worked for several companies considerably larger than the one that said it couldn't use me. In one such case, an executive who had heard me speak brought me in to train all the people in the company who deal regularly with China. Then the same company called me back to be on hand when the chairman of the company met with his Chinese counterpart in a joint venture. I wasn't there as a translator or as a policy maker. They had called me in to do what I do best, which is to make things work.

I have also found that many large firms behave like a huge agglomeration of much smaller firms. Often, executives of such smaller units have problems I can help solve, along with budgets that permit them to hire me. In these cases, it's an advantage for me to be small. Hiring me does not involve the kinds of administrative hassles that are required to obtain the services of my full-service symphonic competitors.

Over time, I've understood that there is some wisdom in what the executive told me. A small firm like mine, or even a slightly larger one, will never have the institutional credibility to tell a huge multinational what its policy should be. But as a talented, imaginative, creative individual I can figure out plenty of ways to serve big clients—and small ones—and make a decent living for myself as I do so.

Bigger or better?

Margaret Gatti's law firm is small and highly specialized. It works for companies and for other law firms solely on international tax, trade, investment and customs issues. One of her clients, she says proudly, is a billion-dollar company.

Margaret has no philosophical objection to expanding her firm, so long as she can maintain close control over the growth and continue to offer high-quality services to her clients. But she believes that getting bigger while staying good is not easy, and she doesn't foresee any significant expansion.

As with many spare room tycoons, Margaret's business is the result of a set of talents and circumstances that are unique to her. "What I do is an accumulation of all I've done," she says.

It is a big step to stand aside from so personal a creation and watch as it inevitably turns into something else. The chief reason for doing so is if you intend to sell your business to someone else, something that doesn't seem to be a high priority for Margaret right now.

She traces her current career back to childhood, as the daughter of a multilingual mother. Margaret had an interest in and aptitude for foreign languages. After getting a master's degree in Germanic studies, she worked briefly for the Library of Congress, and later was hired by the international department of a large bank. The bank paid for her to earn an MBA degree at night, then sent her abroad. She spent the late 1970s working in Germany and Eastern Europe, where she became fascinated by the mechanics and the magic of international trade. One transaction that particularly intrigued her was when she participated with a group of banks that made loans so that Poland could purchase US grain that was fed to pigs that were eventually exported to America in the form of canned hams.

When her bank was absorbed by Mellon Bank, which had a large international department, Margaret was brought back to the US. She continued to work in international trade, dealing not with foreign bankers but with executives of companies that did business overseas. During that time she made 200 or so key contacts who, she says, later made it possible to set up her own business, though she wasn't thinking about it at the time.

Mellon eventually promoted her to be head of its international department, but just as she was settling into her new job, many developing countries were beginning to be delinquent and default on their debt payments. Banks retrenched. Companies that wanted to do international business had difficulty getting loans. Margaret left the bank in 1987, and a few months later she decided to return to school and get a law degree so that she could become an all-around international trade expert.

In order to support herself while she was at law school, Margaret became an entrepreneur. She set up an import–export company, because that was what she knew about. "I always build on what I did in the past," she says, though she adds that during her years as an employee, she never thought about being in business for herself. She did well enough with this business to pay the family bills and the tuition bills. And it gave her confidence, once she earned her law degree, to set up her own firm rather than to go to work for someone else.

"When you are older, you want control over your life," says Margaret, who was 37 when she founded her law firm in 1991. "I wanted to go wherever I wanted to go."

Her firm has done so well that younger lawyers have come to her trying to learn how to replicate her success. She discourages them, saying that the firm worked only because of the knowledge she acquired and the people she came to know before she was a lawyer.

Similarly, her practice is so much the result of her own idiosyncratic career that she has difficulty conceiving of a logical way for it to grow. Two years ago, she says, she took on a lawyer who was also trained as an accountant whom she hoped to train as the firm's specialist in tax matters. It didn't work. Training the new hire was difficult. Margaret wasn't confident of the new lawyer's work and felt she had to check it. "She was a drain on me," Margaret says, and the experiment ended.

She says that a significant advantage of staying small is that big law firms aren't threatened by her, and they feel comfortable making referrals or asking for help. Her fees are lower than theirs because her expenses are lower.

Margaret is busy enough to pick and choose her clients, and she is not forced by high overhead to take on clients with unreasonable expectations or unethical requests. In a career that has had as many twists and turns as hers, it is difficult to predict her course with certainty, but her business will probably remain small. "I'm very happy to stay where I am," she says.

When your business grows up

Sometimes, the market responds so well to your business that you have little choice but to grow. But big expansion brings big changes, and you may find that you're stopped doing what you first set out to do, and have turned into a full-time manager.

That is what has happened to Jennifer Thompson, founder and CEO of LinguaCall, a business that helps Americans deal with foreign languages and culture. She says she is pleased with her firm's growth, and happy as a manager, but the thrill of discovery and creation is gone.

As she tells the story, LinguaCall International happened almost by accident. When Jennifer quit her job as a branch manager of a language and translation company in 1987, she didn't have any idea what she would do. She was 40—too old, she felt, to start over, but without much idea of where she would go. One day, her aunt told her that she wanted to go into business for herself. Jennifer hadn't really considered self-employment, but at that moment, she remembers thinking, "If my aunt can do it, I can do it!"

Then her sister asked Jennifer to translate some material into French. Jennifer did not like to do translations herself, but she knew where to find translators. She decided to start a business finding translators for companies, and offering language instruction to their staffs. The eldest of seven children, she comments that delegating work comes naturally to her.

At first, she called the company Jennifer Thompson, Translation and Language Specialists, but this proved to be a problem. People would ask her which languages she dealt with. When she told them "I can do it all," they were incredulous. In fact, Jennifer wasn't doing all the work herself, but the firm's name implied that she was. She needed a name that put the emphasis on the service she provided, not on herself. A friend suggested that a name she had given to one of her services would be a good name for her business. So LinguaCall it was.

It turned out that she had started her service at an opportune time, one in which several major companies in her area were bought by or merged with European com-

panies. It suddenly became important for American executives to understand what their new, mostly French-
speaking bosses were saying. At just about the time she
renamed her business, she won such a client. Her business
nearly tripled from her second year on the job.

Jennifer had begun her business in a spare bedroom.
She had always used contractors to perform the work, but
now she needed employees to help her manage it. She set
up an office in the basement, then moved a few months
later to an office building. Before long she had a payroll
of 45 full-time and part-time employees and contractors,
working in two different offices.

But even as LinguaCall's business took off, Jennifer
felt depressed. The company was like a child that had
grown up too fast and was now on its own, leaving her
behind. "I don't feel that I am an entrepreneur any more,"
she says. "I'm no longer essential. I feel that I'm working
for LinguaCall, and the company has a life of its own."

She managed to get over her depression fairly
quickly. The separation of LinguaCall from Jennifer
Thompson is, she asserts, a positive thing. It allows her to
keep her own life and identity separate from those of the
company she started.

But she misses the first three years of her business,
the most precarious ones, in which she was scrambling
for clients and improvising services to offer them. She rel-
ishes telling the story of a day when a couple of burly,
cigar-chomping businessmen showed up at her office and
told her they wanted to know enough French to sell steel
to Ivory Coast, in West Africa. "What you need is a con-
versational warm-up course," she told them, making it up
as she spoke. "It will take 100 hours, three times a week."

The businessmen agreed. It was a Thursday, and they wanted to start the following Monday. She spent the weekend recording cassette tapes and creating a manual. The client was happy, and it evolved into one of LinguaCall's most successful products. Running an established business doesn't offer her as many chances to take creative risks, and it's not as much fun.

"One time I had 145 people at an office Christmas party," she recalls. "As I looked at all the people having a good time, I realized that I had made all this happen, and that felt good. But now LinguaCall is living its own life. The name may be worth some money someday, though I don't know how much. But I feel that I'm only working for the company."

Growing too fast

I suppose you could say that the woman I'll call Amy was one of my role models. I first met her when I was teaching at a college in central New York, and she was reinventing herself by starting a new business.

For more than 20 years, Amy and her husband had run a successful business together. The business continued to prosper, but eventually the marriage soured, and they were divorced. Amy had dropped out of college to get married, and she had nothing to fall back on. She clearly contributed to the success of her husband's business. However, after the divorce, though he gave her some money, he still had the business and the contacts and access to borrowing that went along with it. Amy could never amass the capital and goodwill required to start on her own, and besides, once she was out of the business, she came to dislike what they had been doing.

Suddenly alone in middle age, Amy had to figure out what in the world she could do. After a lot of soul searching, and a few false starts, she realized that she was a voracious and sophisticated reader of newspapers and magazines. She noticed by-lines and paid attention to what different writers and television reporters specialized in. Perhaps, she thought, this could serve her well in public relations.

Many publicists work in a scattershot fashion, sending out press releases hit or miss. Amy's was a rifle-like approach. She called specific writers and producers to pitch stories she felt they could hardly refuse. She did it relentlessly. If she was forced to take no for an answer, she had another good idea pretty soon. She came out of nowhere, with no credentials, and in short order was providing the most sophisticated public relations services in her market. I've rarely seen anyone so good at what she does.

I first met her at a party she threw shortly after she started her firm. It was in a glamorous apartment, and there were waiters in white gloves serving champagne and Perrier. Guests didn't see her office, which was in a corner of her bedroom. After a brief apprenticeship, she was launching her own business, and a very impressive group of guests had shown up to wish her well.

We stayed in touch in different cities. By this time, I was in a job I didn't like, and I was, on a not quite conscious level, watching what Amy did. Her business seemed to be prospering. She was always asking me whether I had seen one or another of her clients on *Good Morning America* or in the *Wall Street Journal*. Her client list was growing, and, while she resisted adding to her monthly expenses, it was clear that her business had outgrown her bedroom alcove and her dialing finger.

Her first hire was astute. Amy always felt that her writing wasn't up to the quality of the rest of the services she offered, so she hired a good writer and continued to pitch most of the stories herself. But eventually the business grew large enough that she needed more people and a larger office.

Amy, a believer in projecting a good image, seemed to put more care into the office than into her staff. She believed that because she was offering New York-caliber services, she ought to have a drop-dead environment, and she hired a good architect to achieve it for her. But some of those she hired to work in this stylish, enlarged office couldn't deliver on her implicit promise of brains and sophistication. She was becoming more like any other PR agency.

At around this time, I began my own practice. Amy gave me a great launch present: She got my picture in a prominent magazine with a caption that identified me as an up-and-comer. But she also gave me advice that wasn't really relevant to my business. She told me that I needed to charge much higher rates, to demand long-term commitments and to lay out a strategy for growth. These were things that seemed to be working for her, but she was selling something that's widely desired—fame—while my China business practice appealed to a far smaller and more rarefied clientele. Fortunately, I found some clients soon after I started off, and I was soon very busy, if not very rich.

Suddenly, without explanation, things began to

unravel for Amy. First one contract went unrenewed, then
another, and another. They all told Amy that it was an
internal matter, no reflection on the quality of her work.
Soon her billings were down to where they had been
when she was working alone in her bedroom, but now
she had five mouths to feed and a fancy office to pay for.
She had some good prospects. One always has, and when
things are going bad, they seem to loom even larger and
more golden than before. She told herself that she could-
n't reduce her staff, and there was a lease on the office.
Things were going to come along next month, then the
month after that. But clients never seem to come when
you really need them. She held out for eight months, and
then she was bankrupt.

Shortly before the bankruptcy, I went to her home
for Thanksgiving. (I brought the turkey.) Everything was
festive, but after dinner, she called me into the bedroom
where her business had begun. She lay on the bed, told
me she had failed, and started to cry. I tried to hold her.
She was trembling. She seemed about to explode. She
could not be comforted.

To this day, I don't know why she lost those clients.
Such things happen. But her downfall was not accepting
what had happened, and not adjusting her circumstances
to weather the storm. She recently told me that she feels
her big mistake was to commit to too large an office while
her capital reserves were so small. She said she always
advises others to stay in their bedrooms as long as they
can, and think long and hard before they sign an office
lease. But at the time, she seemed to think that the show-
place office and the staff were affirmations of her success.

Amy is doing fine now, but I still shiver when I think

of what happened to her. And her story reminds me that it's not your overhead, but what's *in* your head, that enables the spare room tycoon to prevail.

Staying small by choice

Gil Gordon is a guru, one of the most often quoted experts on the subject of telecommuting. He has helped some of the world's biggest companies set up programs that allow their employees to work full-time from their homes. But he has ignored all advice to expand his consulting practice by taking on partners or employees, or even franchising it. He is a classic spare room tycoon; he runs his business from the basement of his house in central New Jersey.

Gil is very aware that he has made a choice. He could capitalize on his eminence in this field he helped create by founding an ongoing business that he could some day sell at a profit. "The downside to my not building an empire," he says, "is that I may not be building company assets. My assets are made up of what I know and a stack of papers downstairs."

He knows the choice he is making, and he knows its cost. He also knows its benefits. "Many people have this mystical retirement concept about working like mad and then start enjoying themselves when they retire," he says. "But by the time they turn 65, they have discovered it is too late to enjoy anything. I'd rather enjoy life while doing what I love to do at the same time. What I do today is about lifestyle rather than checkbook."

Shortly before I talked with him, Gil decided to forget the world for a while and disappear into the wilderness, hiking and taking pictures with people he likes. Before he left for the trip, he posted a note on his website saying that he wouldn't be reachable during those days—regardless of the nature of the emergency. "I used to hear this little voice when I was on vacation saying, 'It could be the next million dollar call!' he says. "I have learned to ignore that voice and enjoy the freedom and flexibility that I can afford."

To understand Gil's attitude it's important to know something about the early years of his business. While telecommuting has become widespread in recent years—something that has greatly benefited Gil and his business—it was barely on the radar screen in 1982 when he set up on his own. For quite a few years, Gil's business existed more as an act of will than a response to the market.

Gil describes getting the idea for it almost as an act of defiance. He had first become interested in telecommuting while working as a human resources manager for a diversified consumer products company with operations throughout the world. He saw it as an opportunity to retain talented people and manage employees who need to be on the move.

One day, sometime in the late 1970s, Gil attended a seminar on future employment trends, given by an employee of the US Bureau of Labor Statistics. When one of the participants asked about the prospect of telecommuting, the official gave a dismissive answer. "The idea of telecommuting may be good for a few weirdos or oddballs," he said. "But that's all." Something about that expert's attitude offended Gil deeply. He reflected later that he felt fated to prove the bureaucrat wrong.

This wasn't easy. It took nearly two years from the

time Gil began his practice before he found his first telecommuting client. He opened a bottle of champagne and wrote the name of the client and the date on the cork. But this was not the breakthrough he had hoped for. New telecommuting work was hard to find, and for a couple of years, even the other human resources assignments on which he depended disappeared. He was making less than a waiter, much less than the manager he had once been.

He thought bitterly of what an organizational psychologist who worked for his former boss had told him when he left his employer: "It seems like you're five years ahead of your time," he said. He was haunted and infuriated by those words. He persevered.

In retrospect, it might seem that the psychologist was right. But would Gil's business have become viable if he hadn't spent that time writing, making himself known to journalists and editors, finding audiences for lectures and helping to create the body of opinion required to make what he did into a going enterprise?

"The problem with me in the beginning years was that I was trying to create a market and satisfy it at the same time," he says. He agrees now that it would have been easier to follow the market and offer services whose usefulness was obvious to more people.

But now that he has created a career for himself that works, he has the self-assurance to give his business a shape that fits the life he wants to lead, the confidence to stay small.

❖❖❖

Every business needs to evolve, but not every business

needs to expand, and one should never expand just for expansion's sake. The virtues of the independent life—agility, flexibility, creativity, responsiveness, and personal integrity—tend to diminish as a business grows bigger. And the tasks of management loom larger, which is fine if, and only if, that's where your talents lie.

In nature, plants and animals evolve not to grow larger but to be better adapted to their environment, and that's also the right way to think about the evolution of your business. Your business should be exactly as big as it needs to be to take maximum advantage of both your strengths and the market conditions. While it's not always possible to know this optimum size, you should be worrying about what the proper size is, rather than fretting over when you're going to get larger. Often, the key to surviving bad fortune is well-timed shrinkage.

The best time to think of diversification or change is when you don't need to change. People over the ages have been complaining that we live in a world that is continually changing and that the world is changing too fast.

When I started my business just 17 years ago, the telex machine was the only convenient tool to help companies communicate across borders. Then came the personal computer, the fax machine, the internet and teleconferencing and other new electronic devices that bring people closer. They also make us crazier and crazier. They make us feel that we must do several things at the same time—multitasking—or we're not working productively. The world is changing faster than we can keep up. In this swift-paced world of shrinking national boundaries, no businesses, large or small, are invulnerable, especially those of spare room tycoons.

It is no longer safe to do the same thing over and over again without exploring new territories. We must think ahead and be willing to let go of our own personal myths, goals, romantic visions or corporate missions.

One of my persistent dreams is that I find myself falling from the sky and, in my wish to survive, I tell myself to fly. Then, wings sprout from my shoulders, I start to flap, I stop plummeting and begin to soar. Wishful thinking, no doubt.

But this epitomizes the way of the spare room tycoon as I feel it. There is no security in this world. We can only cope by convincing ourselves that we can't stand still. We must keep transforming ourselves in order to endure and to prosper. We have, after all, invented our lives. The invention can never stop. We must keep rediscovering ourselves and the world we live in. We learn and grow confident. But we never stop starting over.

A Final Thought

It doesn't take much to be a spare room tycoon. It takes a drive to be independent, to carve out a niche in the world for yourself. It takes the courage to choose what you want to become, and to face the ordeals of making it happen. It takes a certain foolhardiness. There's no safety net to catch us if we stumble. Spare room tycoons know this very well. This is why we deserve to rule the kingdoms of our own desire.

Spare room tycoons like you and me do not pretend that we are wealthy or powerful like the real tycoons. This is why we call ourselves spare room tycoons. But because we depend only on ourselves to make a living and no one else, we are subject to no one else on earth. We respect the real tycoons as much as we respect ourselves.

My grandfather really was a tycoon of sorts. At the turn of the twentieth century, when he was in his early teens, he left his village in southern China near Canton. Poor and without anything to his name, he went to Honduras and became very rich. He was the first person in that country to own a private plane. He also owned a lumber yard, a candle import business and a glass factory. He was wealthy enough to retire at age 40. He was a friend of the then president of Honduras. His friend asked him to represent Honduras as its ambassador to China, but he said no. He moved instead to San Francisco.

I got to know him when he was old and had moved back to Hong Kong to live with his eldest son, my father, and his favorite daughter-in-law, my mother; and to die there. I was a small child.

I liked the salami and cheese that my grandfather had shipped to him from America, but I was particularly fascinated by what was written on a parchment scroll. It was one of his prize possessions, protected under glass atop the chest in which he stashed his valuables. I remember climbing up to read the calligraphy.

The parchment was a celebration of industriousness, surmounted by the Chinese character for hard work, written large in bold black brushstrokes. This declaration followed in smaller characters: "I take a walk up the rocky hills with my umbrella open. I see a man who collects firewood. I look at him and see that he is poor. His skin is wrinkled. His feet are sore. I jeer at him for being poor. He looks back at me and says: I make a living on my own. Every grain of rice I eat I earn with my own labor and with a clear conscience. I'm as much of a hero as anyone."

Spare room tycoons need not be wealthy and powerful potentates. We need only be individuals who stand on our own two feet. We search for our heart's desires. We hone our talents and skills. We try to provide some of what the market wants. We make a living on our own, not expecting anyone to feed us. We welcome riches, fame and power if they come. But if they never materialize, we know that we still live our own lives. We are not at anyone's beck and call. We kowtow to nobody.

There will be sunny days and stormy nights, mornings of foggy silence and afternoons of parched desperation. But knowing that we are doing what we want, that we are true to our principles and our talents, and that we answer only to ourselves is a source of joy that will always be with us.

Philadelphia,
January 1, 2000

The 70 Lessons of the Spare Room Tycoon

One of the ways I preserve my own sanity as a spare room tycoon is to keep a diary. In it, I document the struggles, crises, successes and setbacks in my career and my life. When I go back to look at what I have written, I am struck by how often I must rediscover the same truths and recover from the same mistakes. I have found, though, that by writing and rereading my stories, I can save myself some of this wasted energy. The lessons I have recorded serve as signposts that help keep me on track.

This book is, in a sense, a collective diary that recounts the experiences of many. Thus, I thought it would be useful to go through the text and summarize what I think these stories teach.

Some of these lessons are lifted directly from the text, while others distill the insights offered by one or more stories. The lessons are listed in the order that the ideas they convey appear in the book. But because some lessons apply to several stories, while a few stories teach more than one lesson, there is no one-to-one correspondence between the stories and the lessons.

You may find different lessons in these stories, but I think the ones that follow can serve as a checklist to help you look at what you're doing wrong—and doing right.

❖ Being a spare room tycoon is more than a way of making a living, it is a way of living your life.

❖ Spare room tycoons' main payoff comes in personal satisfaction, in autonomy, in deliverance from office politics, in the freedom to make our own mistakes instead of being forced to execute the misjudgments of others.

❖ Discover who you are. You are your business's chief asset.

❖ Passion is a wild card; it transforms and gives power to everything you do.

❖ Who knows how many stillborn businesses there are—possibly very successful ones—that were doomed by a loss of nerve, an unwillingness finally to take action?

❖ Starting a business is an encounter with forces far more powerful than yourself.

❖ Reality rarely, if ever, follows our plans. And although we might be tempted to see that as reality's problem, it's really ours.

❖ Running your business builds confidence and humility—both at the same time. You're surprised by what you've done wrong, and by what you've done right.

❖ Learn to think strategically, not just romantically. Find something that might provide the clue for the next stage of your business.

❖ Believe in your visions, and keep having new ones.

Starting

- ❖ Identify your strengths and design your business around them.
- ❖ The spark for a successful business is as likely to come from your personal life as from your professional one.
- ❖ When you do what you love, the money doesn't necessarily follow. You have to be doing something that people value highly enough to provide the level of income you require.
- ❖ No matter how carefully you have tried to plan, things won't work out as you expected.
- ❖ When things don't work, don't panic. Figure out why. When good results come from areas where you weren't expecting them, listen to what the market is telling you.
- ❖ Get over getting fired, then worry about your business plan.
- ❖ Expect to fail a few times.
- ❖ You never know where the money will come from.
- ❖ Forget who you used to be.

Succeeding

- ❖ Selling is like breathing: Stop and your business dies.
- ❖ Promoting your business isn't just for bad times. And it's not just for good times. It is for all times.
- ❖ You're promoting your business, not yourself. If you learn to make the distinction, it is easier to sell and not so devastating to be turned down.
- ❖ Small customers have money too.
- ❖ Be prepared to be successful. A business plan is useful,

but if it's too restrictive, it can blind you to opportunities that you're well equipped to realize.

❖ Opportunities are often what we define them to be. Spare room tycoons are frequently faced not with well-defined challenges, but with ambiguous situations. What we make of such chances can alter everything.

❖ When people want you, they'll find a reason to value you. But when you're trying to sell your services to people who are not ready to use them, you'll never win regardless of how logical, useful, valuable, or perfect you are.

❖ Sometimes you win despite yourself.

❖ One of the most powerful things you can do is to be out and about, reminding people you're still in business.

❖ Your first client is yourself.

❖ Confidence is money. Self-worth can translate into net worth.

❖ Build confidence like a muscle, by facing anxieties, meeting challenges, and discovering that you have lived to tell the tale.

❖ Business is a contact sport. Looking, acting and feeling sure of yourself gives you a big edge.

❖ Ask for what you need to do a good job.

❖ Determine what risks you can live with, then take them.

❖ A brand is a distillation of identity and an affirmation of quality. Big companies use brands to give their products attributes that most spare room tycoons already possess.

❖ Stay true to what makes you unique.

❖ Most people dress to belong. The spare room tycoon must dress to bill.

❖ Don't pretend to be something you're not. But create a good package for all that you are.

❖ While developing your business is the most important thing in your life, it isn't the most important thing in anybody else's life.

❖ If you want people to help you, don't see them as targets.

❖ Being known as someone people can depend on is the best promotion of all.

❖ Charge enough to live. If you don't, you won't have a business.

❖ Part of pricing is a science. The rest is confidence in action.

❖ To justify your price, numbers are stronger than self-esteem.

❖ Your billing must be timely and clear, or you will spend your life in a cashflow squeeze.

❖ Serve your customers well. Don't count on being loved.

Sustaining

❖ Seek a sane balance between work and life.

❖ When you become your own boss, learn not to be a slave-driver.

❖ Your business won't succeed if you die trying.

❖ When you become independent, you realize how much you count on others.

❖ To be able to ignore a ringing telephone is the beginning of sanity.

❖ Find your business a room of its own.

❖ Stay in touch with people you like.

❖ Other people's anxieties are what keep us in business.

❖ Choose the anxieties you can live with.

❖ Anxieties are less troublesome when we're busy. A regular routine helps keep them at bay.

❖ Don't let crazy customers drive you mad.

❖ There are few things that cause more anxiety than the aspiration to safety; suddenly everything life throws at you jeopardizes your illusion of security.

❖ Rejoice in good times, have faith in bad times.

❖ Survival itself is reason to celebrate.

❖ To sustain yourself, you must sometimes make painful compromises.

❖ Even if you encounter the ghost of failure, don't let it haunt you.

❖ Sometimes the worst happens. That's when you have to do something else.

❖ Apparent disaster may hold the seeds of future success.

❖ Every business needs to evolve, but not every business needs to expand.

❖ You can't make a plant grow by pulling on it.

❖ It's not your overhead, but what's *in* your head that counts.

❖ You don't need to change your size to change the world.

❖ When your business expands, you have to become a manager.

❖ Spare room tycoons want freedom and independence. Building an ever-expanding empire is optional.

Spare Room Tycoon grew from a sharing of stories. I hope that these conversations can be expanded to include the book's readers. If you have stories or lessons that you want to share with other spare room tycoons, visit my website at http://www.spareroomtycoon.com.

You can also write to me at:

Asia Marketing and Management

2014 Naudain Street

Philadelphia, PA 19146-1317

USA

Email: asiamark@pipeline.com

Acknowledgments

I would like to thank my fellow spare room tycoons who helped make this book possible. They have given me their personal stories—emotional, psychological or practical skills and insights that make them successful in what they do. They are, in alphabetical order by family name, Carol Aitken, Marilyn Bellock, Robert J. Booker, Margaret R. Brogan, John Austin Carey, Brett Cohen, Rocky Condino, Ruth Dalphin, Denise L. Devine, Joseph S. Dolan, Aram Fox, William T. Frysinger, Margaret M. Gatti, Gil Gordon, Ralf Graves, Stan Gross, Martha E. Hughes, Alan J. Kaplan, Sam Maitin, Frances McElroy, Michael McGrail, Thys van der Merwe, Rochana and Richard Norby, Janet M. Opdyke, Christina Pirello, Gary R. Samartino, Mariann E. Schick, Erick R. Schilling, Marvin Schwam, Stephen B. Sherretta, Richard A. Signorelli, Mario Sikora, Helen H. Solomons, Jeff Tannenbaum, Ellen E. Thompson, Jennifer C. Thompson, and Bill Wollheim.

I would like to thank Ann Cornell, Karen Davies, Eric Dietrich, Virginia Cairo Elwell, Peter Lantos, Sizostris Makar, Marthe Roberts/Shea and Lauri Ward for granting me interviews. They are all very successful business men and women who generously shared their insights with me.

I would like to thank Steven Halin for the right to use his photograph of me.

Thanks to my client and friend, Thomas G. DiRenzo, for reading parts of the manuscript and for giving me many valuable suggestions.

Thanks to Louise DiRenzo, Douglas Atterbury, Jeff Coble, Allison Jones and Doug Tharp for introducing me to several of the spare room tycoons in this book.

I am grateful to my literary agent, Liv Blumer, and to her associate Barney Karpfinger for their support and guidance.

I would like to thank my publisher Nick Brealey of Nicholas Brealey Publishing, who believes in the way of the spare room tycoon. Thanks also to Sally Lansdell for her judicious and expeditious editing.

Finally, this book would never have been written without the inspiration and help of Thomas Hine. He was the first to call me a "spare room tycoon."

Index